# MRS. PACKARD

# MRS. PACKARD

*Inspired by a True Story*

## Emily Mann

THEATRE COMMUNICATIONS GROUP
NEW YORK
2009

*Mrs. Packard* is published by Theatre Communications Group, Inc., 520 Eighth Avenue, 24th Floor, New York, NY 10018–4156

This publication is made possible in part with public funds from the New York State Council on the Arts, a State Agency.

TCG books are exclusively distributed to the book trade by Consortium Book Sales and Distribution.

LIBRARY OF CONGRESS CATALOGING-IN-PUBLICATION DATA
Mann, Emily.
Mrs. Packard : a play inspired by a true story / Emily Mann.—1st ed.
p. cm.
ISBN 978-1-55936-334-1 (alk. paper)
I. Title.
PS3563.A5357M77 2008
812'.54—dc22    2008053445

Cover design by Carol Devine Carson
Text design and composition by Lisa Govan

First Edition, May 2009

Much madness is divinest sense
To a discerning eye;
Much sense the starkest madness.
'Tis the majority
In this, as all, prevails.
Assent, and you are sane;
'Demur,—you're straightaway
dangerous,
And handled with a chain.

—*Emily Dickinson*

# MRS. PACKARD

## Production History

*Mrs. Packard* received its world premiere in May 2007 at the
McCarter Theatre Center (Emily Mann, Artistic Director/Resi-
dent Playwright; Jeffrey Woodward, Managing Director) in
Princeton, NJ. It was subsequently produced in June 2007 at
The Kennedy Center in Washington, D.C., with the same
artistic staff and cast. It was directed by Emily Mann, the set
design was by Eugene Lee, the costume design was by Jennifer
von Mayrhauser, the lighting design was by Jeff Croiter, origi-
nal music and sound design were by Rob Milburn and
Michael Bodeen, the fight direction was by Rick Sordelet,
movement direction was by Peter Pucci, dramaturgy was by
Douglas Langworthy; the production stage manager was
Cheryl Mintz. The cast was as follows:

| | |
|---|---|
| ELIZABETH PARSONS WARE PACKARD | Kathryn Meisle |
| REVEREND THEOPHILUS PACKARD | John C. Vennema |
| DR. ANDREW MCFARLAND | Dennis Parlato |
| MRS. BONNER | Fiana Toibin |
| MRS. TENNEY, MRS. SYBIL DOLE | Julie Boyd |
| MRS. CHAPMAN, MISS SARAH RUMSEY, MRS. BLESSING | Molly Regan |
| MRS. STOCKTON | Georgine Hall |

MR. JOSEPHUS SMITH, MR. HASLET,
MR. BLACKMAN AND OTHERS      Robin Chadwick

DR. J. W. BROWN, MR. ABIJAH DOLE,
DR. DUNCANSON AND OTHERS      Jeff Brooks

ENSEMBLE      Karen Christie-Ward,
Beth Dzuricky,
Mitchell Michaliszyn,
Quinn Warren,
Ray Wiederhold

# Characters

MRS. ELIZABETH PARSONS WARE PACKARD

REVEREND THEOPHILUS PACKARD, her husband

DR. ANDREW MCFARLAND, superintendent of Jacksonville

MRS. BONNER, matron at Jacksonville

MRS. TENNEY, matron of the 8th Ward; MRS. SYBIL DOLE, witness for the prosecution

MRS. CHAPMAN, patient of the 7th Ward; MISS SARAH RUMSEY, witness for the prosecution; MRS. BLESSING, witness for the defense

MRS. STOCKTON, patient of the 7th Ward

JUDGE; MR. JOSEPHUS SMITH, witness for the prosecution; MR. HASLET, counsel for the prosecution; DR. CHRISTOPHER W. KNOTT, witness for the prosecution; MR. LA BRIE, witness for the defense; MR. BLACKMAN, president of the board of trustees

CLERK; MR. STEPHEN R. MOORE, counsel for the defense; DR. J. W. BROWN, witness for the prosecution; MR. ABIJAH DOLE, witness for the prosecution; DR. DUNCANSON, expert witness for the defense; MR. BLESSING, witness for the defense; FOREMAN OF THE JURY

ARTHUR, the Packards' young son

### ENSEMBLE:

ATTENDANT; TRUSTEE

LIBBY, 8th ward inmate

ELEGANT LADY OF THE 8TH WARD

VIOLENT LADY OF THE 8TH WARD

*Note: Four males and five females, in addition to a few ensemble members, play all the roles. Suggestions for doubling are detailed above.*

## Setting

Illinois, 1861–1864. The stage serves as a theatrical space that becomes many places.

Married women and infants who, in the judgment of the medical superintendent are evidently insane or distracted, may be entered or detained in the hospital on the request of the husband of the woman or the guardian of the infant, without the evidence of insanity required in other cases.

*—The State of Illinois,*
*Passed into law on February 15, 1851*

# ACT ONE

✑✑

*Illinois 1861 and 1864. A theatrical space that will become many places. A grated window. Bolted doors.*
*Tight white light up on the Judge.*

JUDGE: The case on trial at Kankakee City, Illinois, January 11, 1864. Upon the motion of the Honorable Charles B. Starr, presiding, it is ordered that an issue be formed as to the sanity or insanity of Mrs. Elizabeth P. W. Packard, and that a jury of twelve men will aid in the investigation of said issue. The court will come to order in the matter of *Packard v. Packard.*

*(Sound of a gavel. The lights change to Dr. McFarland's office. 1861. Jacksonville Insane Asylum. Reverend Theophilus Packard, fifty-seven, is with Dr. McFarland, a good-looking forty-five. Theophilus is very upset.)*

DR. MCFARLAND: And who will care for your children, Reverend Packard, now that your wife will be confined?

THEOPHILUS: My sister lives near us and though she has children of her own, she—she offered . . . *(Dr. McFarland: "I see.")* And some of the women in my congregation offered to—to help as well *(Choking)* and the older children will—

DR. MCFARLAND: Yes . . . I'm sure.

THEOPHILUS: Can you help my wife, Doctor?

DR. MCFARLAND: I will know more after my examination of her . . .

THEOPHILUS: Yes, yes. Of course.

DR. MCFARLAND: But cases like your wife's are a specialty of mine here at Jacksonville. *(Theophilus, hoarsely: "Really?")* Tell me, though, Reverend, are you quite certain you have tried every avenue with your wife to keep her calm?

THEOPHILUS: I do not know what else to do! It is very difficult for me to leave her here, but I fear for the children's spiritual and—and physical welfare. *(Dr. McFarland: "I see.")* She flies into rages, Doctor. I can no longer control her, and I fear I now may lose my present church.

DR. MCFARLAND: Your "present church"? Has this happened before, sir?

THEOPHILUS *(Beside himself)*: Oh, yes. We have had to move three times in the last ten years due to my wife's—outbursts. I—I love my wife, Doctor. Before that, she was a—a good wife and mother and a help-mate to me in my church, but *now* I—I—

*(There is a knock on the door. Mrs. Bonner, an Irish matron, sticks her head in.)*

MRS. BONNER: Doctor?

DR. MCFARLAND: Mrs. Bonner.

MRS. BONNER: I have Mrs. Packard with me. Shall I bring her in?

DR. MCFARLAND: Yes, yes . . . Reverend, please remain quiet during my examination of your wife. She may be upset, but let me handle—

*(Elizabeth, forty-three, and very beautiful, enters, hair flying, in a rage. She pulls away from Mrs. Bonner.)*

ELIZABETH: Don't you touch me! *(Seeing Theophilus; spitting this at him)* "Peter, Peter, pumpkin eater, had a wife and couldn't keep her . . ." *(She continues over the others)*

DR. MCFARLAND *(Overlapping)*: Mrs. Packard?

THEOPHILUS *(Overlapping)*: Elizabeth, don't . . . *(Gets up)*

ELIZABETH: "Put her in a pumpkin shell."

THEOPHILUS *(Overlapping)*: Stop it.

ELIZABETH: "And there he kept her very well."

*(A pause. She and Theophilus look at each other. Silence. Theophilus turns away.)*

DR. MCFARLAND: Mrs. Packard? I am Doctor Andrew McFarland, Superintendent of Jacksonville Insane Asylum. *(Elizabeth: "Oh?")* I should like to have a discussion with you, Mrs. Packard, with your husband present before he leaves you here with us. *(Elizabeth: "But, Doctor—")* I wish to assure you—you will be quite comfortable here . . . And will in future be in my . . . personal care.

*(Their eyes meet.)*

ELIZABETH *(Suddenly girlish, almost flirtatious)*: Really? I am so glad to hear it—that I would be in your personal care. However, you must surely see I don't belong here! *(Dr. McFarland: "Ah, yes?")* Yes! I don't know why it is, Doctor—it may be merely a foolish pride—but I can't help feeling an instinctive aversion to being called insane. *(Pause)* Like Peter Peter's wife? She felt the same, I'm sure—living in a pumpkin shell . . .

DR. MCFARLAND *(Unsure, almost a laugh)*: . . . Indeed . . . *(Offers her a seat)* Your husband and I have had a long talk this morning *(Elizabeth, bitterly: "Have you?")* and he tells me that you love to read and write and discuss . . .

ELIZABETH *(Wary)*: Yes . . . Quite right.

DR. MCFARLAND: Well, I intend for you to enjoy special privileges while you are here with us *(Elizabeth: "No, no—")* and I will be sure to furnish you with books of your choosing. *(Elizabeth: "But, Doctor—")* Perhaps you and I will be able to converse together as well. I should like that.

*(A moment. Then Elizabeth bolts, runs toward her husband, starts to whale on him.)*

ELIZABETH: I will not! Stay! Here! I will not stay! Why are you turning everybody against me? Why are you trying to convince anyone who'll listen I am mad?!

DR. MCFARLAND *(Overlapping)*: Mrs. Packard! Mrs. Packard! Please take your seat. Mrs. Packard! . . .

*(Dr. McFarland stops her from hitting her husband.)*

Please take a seat and let us finish our interview in a civilized manner.

*(Dr. McFarland sits her back down.)*

ELIZABETH *(Muttering, shaking her head, laughing at the absurdity, spitting at her husband)*: "Peter, Peter, pumpkin eater—had a wife . . ."

DR. MCFARLAND: Now, then—

ELIZABETH *(Laughing to herself)*: The children's favorite rhyme . . .

DR. MCFARLAND: I do hope you slept well and that the plain food of the asylum will agree with you.

ELIZABETH *(Snaps)*: No, I am afraid nothing "agrees with me" here. None of this "agrees with me." *(Dr. McFarland: "I'm sorry . . .")* Quite frankly, my bed is narrow and hard and made of straw and I am unused to sleeping alone.

*(Theophilus shifts uncomfortably. Dr. McFarland looks up and smiles.)*

DR. MCFARLAND: . . . I understand.

ELIZABETH: In fact, when I ceased, only recently, to have the warmth of my once dear husband in bed beside me, I brought the youngest of my children into bed with me so that I could sleep. This my husband well knows. So, no, I did not sleep well, I thank you. I could not.

DR. MCFARLAND: How many children do you have, Mrs. Packard?

ELIZABETH: We have six children, five boys and a girl. *(Tears start to stream)* The oldest is eighteen years old and the youngest eighteen *months. (To Theophilus)* All except the oldest were living at home the morning I was abducted.

DR. MCFARLAND: "Abducted"?

ELIZABETH *(Trying to keep the hysteria and sobs down)*: Yes, "abducted"! I was having my bath—I—I looked out the window—saw a sheriff . . . and two strong men, two doctors . . . and my husband!—walk—come walking up the path to our front door, up the stairs . . . yelling, pounding on my—my bedroom door! . . . I screamed I—I wasn't dressed. They would not wait! They . . . hacked down the door—with an ax. Completely . . . naked!!! Terrified—as any woman would be . . .

DR. MCFARLAND: Surely.

ELIZABETH: A doctor took my hand. "Her pulse is very quick!" he said . . . And pronounced me insane. The second doctor, the—the same . . . My husband . . . said: "Get dressed. At once!" Then two strong men carried me out of my house . . . onto a . . . a waiting wagon!! Then onto a—train . . . here. *(Pause )* I was . . . abducted . . . Don't you agree?

DR. MCFARLAND *(Nods)*: I see you did not come on your own volition, Mrs. Packard.

*(Pause.)*

ELIZABETH *(In a small voice)*: Doctor . . . I try—

DR. MCFARLAND *(Gently taking her hand)*: Mrs. Packard, you are here because your husband is concerned about your sanity, and wants you to have professional care.

ELIZABETH: . . . Doctor . . . my husband is jealous! *(Theophilus: "Now, wait just one . . .")* His congregation is dwindling. I—I encouraged . . . healthy discussion! . . . The Christ I worship and love would not have an innocent baby *damned at birth*, Theophilus! *(Screaming at her husband)* It is woman who will crush the serpent's head!—

THEOPHILUS: That is quite enough, Mrs. Packard! You see, Doctor? This is what I was telling you. She flies into these fits frequently. This is what I have been living with and—

DR. MCFARLAND *(Gently signals him to calm down)*: Yes, Mr. Packard . . . Mrs. Packard, I understand you . . . flouted your husband in front of his congregation?

*(Long pause.)*

THEOPHILUS: She did.

ELIZABETH *(Very quiet)*: . . . I did . . . ask for the congregation and the minister's blessing to leave the church and worship with the Methodists . . .

DR. MCFARLAND *(Amazed, almost amused)*: You made this request during Sunday service? Your husband was at the pulpit?

THEOPHILUS: Yes. I was at the pulpit. She exposed her perversity to full public view! *(Dr. McFarland: "Ah.")* The entire congregation saw she had gone mad.

ELIZABETH: Since neither you nor the congregation responded to my request, I left the church and crossed the street to worship with the Methodists! . . . *(Whispers to Dr. McFarland)* . . . where my personal beliefs could be respected.

DR. MCFARLAND: How long ago did you interrupt your husband's service, Mrs. Packard?

ELIZABETH: . . . Nine weeks ago.

DR. MCFARLAND: I see. And how long would you say these disagreements about religion have caused—marital strife— between you and your husband?

ELIZABETH: The last year or so, I should think, but it's not only religion, Doctor, it's—

THEOPHILUS *(Interrupting; erupting)*: The last *ten* years, at least, Elizabeth!!! *(Elizabeth looks at him aghast)* Her mother was mad as well, Doctor, you should know, and Mrs. Packard herself was committed to an asylum once before, when she was young.

ELIZABETH: I was put in hospital for brain fever!—not madness! My father will attest to that. *(Theophilus: "Nonsense.")* . . . And my mother was not mad, Doctor. She had lost four children in infancy, and she did *grieve* for them. *(Dr. McFarland: "Of course." Spitting at her husband)* She doubtless wept because she'd been taught her babies were damned for eternity!

THEOPHILUS: You see?! . . . As I told you, Doctor, it is a clear case of moral perversity.

DR. MCFARLAND *(Slowly)*: Yes, most insanity starts as such, but often we can find a cure, *(To Elizabeth)* if the patient is willing. *(He rises)* Reverend, I leave you with your wife to say good-bye . . . *(The men look at one another)* Mrs. Packard, let me remind you that you will have every special privilege here while under my watch.

*(She offers her hand to Dr. McFarland in gratitude. He holds it for a moment, looking deeply into her eyes.)*

ELIZABETH: Doctor.

DR. MCFARLAND: It has been a . . . very great pleasure to meet you, Mrs. Packard. Truly.

*(He then nods to Theophilus as he exits, leaving Elizabeth with her husband. There is a long silence. Neither speaks. Then with great control:)*

ELIZABETH *(Smiling)*: You see, Husband? The doctor does not think me mad.

THEOPHILUS: You are wrong there, Mrs. Packard. Believe me.

*(The lights change.*
*Mr. Smith, dressed all in black, testifies.)*

CLERK: Mr. Josephus Smith, you have been sworn.

MR. SMITH: I have been in charge of the Bible school at Reverend Packard's church since just before Mrs. Packard was taken to the asylum three years ago. I was elected superintendent of the school for the special purpose of keeping Mrs. Packard *straight*. We all knew—the entire congregation knew—Mrs. Packard was insane. She thought she was the Holy Ghost . . .

*(The lights change.)*

ELIZABETH *(Quiet)*: Theophilus, how can you do this to the mother of your children?

THEOPHILUS: It is for your own good—and quite obviously—for the good of the children.

ELIZABETH: What will the children do without their mother?

THEOPHILUS: My sister will help and Libby will be helpful as well.

ELIZABETH: Libby is only ten years old, Theo. She's a little girl!

THEOPHILUS: I am well aware of her age, Mrs. Packard. The children will be well cared for, and they will soon get used to it.

ELIZABETH: They will not "get used to it" and neither shall I!

THEOPHILUS: You are very ill, Elizabeth, and you are harming the children.

ELIZABETH: I am not *ill*, Husband, and well you know it! *(Pause)* I—I understand. You are angry . . . It was a great betrayal and a great humiliation, *(Beside herself)* but—but you never listen!!! or or . . . care to—or or . . . let me *think*!— and I—I—for *myself*!! and—

THEOPHILUS: Stop babbling.

ELIZABETH: Theo! Let us talk at home, in the privacy of our home.

THEOPHILUS: I gave you fair warning.

ELIZABETH: This is a prison, Theo! I am begging you. The matron threw me to the floor this morning! Theo, please. I shall *die* here.

*(Mrs. Bonner listens outside the door.)*

THEOPHILUS: You're hysterical. Sit down. I don't want them to have to restrain you again.

ELIZABETH: Dear God, I shall die without my babies. It's the reason I'm alive, Theo, to be a mother, to care for my little ones. *(He puts his head in his hands)* Don't you have any tender feelings left for me? I slept in your bed for twenty-one years, I bore you six beautiful children, I kept a spotless, loving Christian home for you. Please take me home. I will be forever in your debt. I'll do anything, anything. Please, Theo! Theo, I'm begging you. *(She looks closer)* Are you asleep? . . .

THEOPHILUS: I'm sorry. I have been broken of my rest.

ELIZABETH *(Laughing and crying)*: . . . You "have been broken of your rest"!? *(She pulls herself together)* I see . . .

THEOPHILUS *(Sad)*: I hope some day you will understand . . . I had no recourse. You endanger the souls of your family and yourself as you are now. *(Gently taking her hand)* As

*16*

I have told you repeatedly, you may think your own thoughts, Elizabeth, when you are thinking right; and once you are thinking right, you may return home. *(He thinks of embracing her but she turns from him)* I sincerely hope . . . you will be cured.

*(He exits. Elizabeth starts sobbing. Mrs. Bonner enters to guard her, watches her in turmoil.)*

MRS. BONNER: Ye didn't get yer way, didja? You fancy ladies never do.

ELIZABETH: I thank you to keep your opinions to yourself.

MRS. BONNER: Oh, wouldja now?

ELIZABETH: He's the crazy one. Not me.

MRS. BONNER: But he's the one leavin', darling, livin' in the world.

*(The lights change.*
*Mrs. Dole, a woman in a black bonnet, is on the witness stand.)*

MR. HASLET: State your name please for the record.

MRS. DOLE: I am Mrs. Sybil Dole, Mr. Packard's sister.

MR. HASLET: Mrs. Dole—did you ever see your sister-in-law behave in a manner that made you think her mad?

MRS. DOLE *(With great indignation)*: Yes. One evening we were sitting at table . . .

*(The lights change. Bell sounds for breakfast. Women enter, pushing on two tables with them. Simultaneous scenes:)*

MRS. BONNER: All right! Come on, ladies. Step to it! *(She takes out a stick from her belt and slams it on the table)*

MRS. DOLE: Mrs. Packard was talking about religion.

MRS. BONNER: You! The new girl! *(She points to Elizabeth)* Over there.

*(Elizabeth goes where she is directed: a table with two other women. Both are neat and middle class. Mrs. Stockton, seventy, picks at the dry food in front of her. She smiles at Elizabeth. Mrs. Chapman, forty, greets her with a nod. Elizabeth whispers a question to her.)*

MRS. DOLE: She became very excited. When Mr. Packard remonstrated with her, she became extremely angry . . .

MRS. BONNER *(To Elizabeth)*: No talkin'!

MRS. DOLE: She rose up from the table, said she would have "no fellowship with the unfruitful work of darkness" . . . took her teacup, and left the room in great violence.

*(A violent woman from the 8th Ward table starts screaming. She bangs and waves her cup. She runs over to Elizabeth and tries to hit her with her cup.)*

MRS. BONNER: Stop that, ya little tit!

*(Mrs. Bonner restrains the woman and starts to beat her and kick her into submission. The others make a racket.)*

Silence! Eat yer food. And sit up straight alla yas. Or you'll grow hunchbacked like the *auld* ladies sittin' over there! *(Indicates Elizabeth's table)* You wouldn't want to look like any o' them now, wouldja?

*(She laughs. She saunters over to Elizabeth's table, and stops behind her.)*

*(To the 8th Ward table)* What do we think of the new girl? She looks a bit *waek* to me. *(To Elizabeth)* Are you the *waek* one, Mrs. Packard? *(Pause)* Don't answer right now. Think on it. We'll talk tomorrow . . . and the day after that. I'll check up on ya . . . Every day . . .

*(Mrs. Bonner moves on. The women at Elizabeth's table show her sympathy. Mrs. Chapman pats Elizabeth's hand. Elizabeth stares at her.)*

*Quiet!* Alla yas. Now EAT!

*(Mrs. Bonner slams her stick down. They eat the dry food in silence.*

*The lights change. Mrs. Dole's testimony continues as the formation of the 7th Ward, Elizabeth's ward, takes shape onstage.)*

MR. HASLET: Mrs. Dole, do you believe your sister-in-law was insane? Or is insane?

MRS. DOLE: I do. Mrs. Packard would not think to leave the Church *unless* she was insane.

MR. MOORE *(The defense; interrupting)*: Mrs. Dole, do you believe literally that Elijah went direct up to Heaven in a chariot of fire—

MRS. DOLE: I do.

MR. MOORE: That the chariot had wheels, and seats, and was driven by horses?

MRS. DOLE: I do.

MR. MOORE: Do you believe Jonah was swallowed by a whale and remained in its belly three days and then was cast up?!

MRS. DOLE *(With great clarity)*: It is in the Bible, sir.

*(The lights change. It is a week later in the 7th Ward.*
    *Mrs. Bonner enters, pushing a very large trunk. We hear*
*a woman crying in an adjacent ward.)*

MRS. BONNER: Yer husband sent you this, Mrs. Packard.

ELIZABETH: Oh, thank heavens.

*(She runs to the trunk and opens it. She rummages through*
*the contents.)*

MRS. BONNER *(Laughing)*: Judgin' by the size of it, he expects
    yer stayin' till Doomsday!

*(Elizabeth takes out old "doing her chores" clothes. She*
*finds some rotten fruit. She digs further, frantic.)*

ELIZABETH: Is this some kind of a cruel joke?! *(She digs to the*
    *bottom)* Mrs. Bonner, is this all there is for me? None of
    my good clothes? . . . No paper or pen?

MRS. BONNER: That's what came last week, whatcha have there.

ELIZABETH: There must be some notes or tokens from my
    children.

MRS. BONNER: And why would good little children want to be
    writin' a crazy lady in the nuthouse, Mrs. Packard.

ELIZABETH *(Stung)*: Excuse me—?

MRS. BONNER: You heard me.

ELIZABETH *(Shaking with anger, but with lady-like force)*:
    Mrs. Bonner, may I please have some paper and a pen?!

MRS. BONNER: No . . . No . . . that's all ya got in the wide world,
    what you have there. Don't know what else to tell ya . . .
    He's *your* husband, thank God, not mine! *(She exits,*
    *amused)*

*(Elizabeth goes back to the trunk and continues to look through it. She pulls out an old mirror and stares at her reflection. She sits, humiliated. Mrs. Chapman comes over to her.)*

MRS. CHAPMAN: You'll find a way to survive, dear. Give it time.

*(Elizabeth closes her eyes. She shoves away the mirror. The tears flow.)*

ELIZABETH: How long have you been here?
MRS. CHAPMAN: 3,446 days. But who counts days?
ELIZABETH: Nearly ten years? *(Her voice rising)* Dear God.
MRS. CHAPMAN: I never agreed to do what my husband wanted, you see. So he's kept me here. I wouldn't be surprised if I die here.
ELIZABETH: You chose to stay?
MRS. CHAPMAN: Yes, I suppose . . . In the end.
ELIZABETH: Do you have children?
MRS. CHAPMAN: . . . No.

*(Elizabeth gets up.)*

ELIZABETH: Well I have to get out of here. My children need me . . . *(Paces)*
MRS. CHAPMAN: Of course they do.

*(Elizabeth looks at her in panic.)*

ELIZABETH: I am not mad.
MRS. CHAPMAN *(An odd laugh)*: You see the woman in the corner there sleeping? She's a spiritualist. She actually fore-

saw the War Between the States, but she talked about it.
She's an abolitionist. Her husband is not. Mrs. Stockton
there? Her husband is a minister, very old school . . .
*(Elizabeth nods: "Ah . . . Yes . . ." Mrs. Chapman takes note)*
She started studying with a Swedenborgianist about ten
years ago. Her husband would not have it. And the
woman in the corner there? She and her husband . . . "dis-
agreed" about her property, so . . .

ELIZABETH: But Doctor McFarland does not think *I'm* mad.

MRS. CHAPMAN *(An odd laugh)*: Mrs. Packard! Make no mis-
take, dear. You're here because the doctor has agreed to
keep you here. In my experience—

*(Dr. McFarland enters with Mrs. Bonner.)*

DR. MCFARLAND: Good morning, ladies. Mrs. Bonner will
take you to the yard while I treat Mrs. Packard.

*(Mrs. Chapman looks at her, alarmed. Mrs. Bonner gath-
ers together the women and takes them out, as Elizabeth
tries to compose herself.)*

MRS. BONNER: Step lively, ladies, you heard the doctor! Come
on, now! Move quickly, Mrs. Chapman! Or I'll lose my
patience with ya. Mrs. Stockton, I'll knock yer carcass
from here to kingdom come if ya don't move along. Holy
Joseph!! Git on with ye!

*(They exit.)*

DR. MCFARLAND: And how are you feeling today?

ELIZABETH: Oh . . . m-much better . . . now that you are with me, Doctor . . . *(He smiles)* As you know . . . I don't belong here.

DR. MCFARLAND: . . . You look a bit calmer than you did on first meeting.

ELIZABETH: . . . Perhaps the shock . . . of my abduction . . . is beginning to wear off . . .

DR. MCFARLAND: Good. Now, what books shall I bring you, Mrs. Packard? I promised you in our interview I would furnish you with books of your choosing.

ELIZABETH: Well . . . though I do enjoy reading a vast . . . array of—of theologians, I—do not think I'll be here long enough to start a new and weighty volume, Doctor, *(In a small voice)* do you? *(He smiles)* . . . Perhaps a newspaper? So I can follow the progress . . . of our Union troops . . .

DR. MCFARLAND *(Surprised, impressed)*: Really? Easily done . . . You must know, Mrs. Packard, I have met many intelligent and learned women in my day, but they were rarely married. Rarely mothers.

ELIZABETH: Yes, well . . . my father thought it only just that I have the same opportunities to cultivate my mind as my brothers.

DR. MCFARLAND: You're a fortunate woman.

ELIZABETH: Yes, well, my father is an extraordinary man. When I was a little girl, I would sit outside his study door for hours, and listen to the guests who came to visit . . . fellow ministers like my father or . . . or eminent scholars. I love to learn. *(Tears start to stream)*

DR. MCFARLAND: Yes . . .

ELIZABETH: And I often had lively conversations with my father . . . about these new ideas . . . I always longed to with my— *(Stops herself)*

DR. MCFARLAND: I'm sorry.

*(He gives her his handkerchief. She takes it.)*

There, there . . . breathe deeply . . . just be still for a moment.

ELIZABETH: I . . . Yes, Doctor.

*(Long pause.)*

DR. MCFARLAND: I should like to give you a new treatment, Mrs. Packard, to relieve some of your strain. You will feel my hands. Just breathe deeply. Your nervous system has been severely taxed . . .

ELIZABETH: Yes, *(Whispers)* yes, it has.

DR. MCFARLAND: . . . Breathe deeply, Mrs. Packard . . . That's it . . .

*(He gently starts to place his hands on her back. She has not been touched in weeks. She starts to breathe deeply and enjoys the touch.)*

Feel the warmth of my hands . . . *(Elizabeth: "Oh . . .")* Yes . . . shhhh . . . shhhh . . . on your back . . . and your neck . . . and your shoulders.

ELIZABETH: Yes . . .

DR. MCFARLAND: You can trust me, Mrs. Packard.

ELIZABETH: Yes . . .

DR. MCFARLAND: Just breathe deeply . . . *(Elizabeth: "Ah . . .")* And feel my hands on your back and your neck . . . And your throat . . . And your chest . . .

ELIZABETH: Ah!

DR. MCFARLAND: Just relax ... Your lower back and your chest ... You're trembling, Elizabeth ...

ELIZABETH: Yes ...

DR. MCFARLAND: Just give in ... That's it ... Just ... give ... in ... Close your eyes, feel my warmth ... Shhh ... shhh. There ... There ...

ELIZABETH: Ah ... Ah ...

DR. MCFARLAND: Yes, yes ... Yes ...

ELIZABETH: Ahhhh ...

*(A long silence.)*

DR. MCFARLAND: You may open your eyes now, Mrs. Packard.

*(She opens her eyes, looks around dazed, trembling and flushed.)*

How do you feel now? You look very much better.

ELIZABETH: ... Yes! ... I feel ... very much better.

DR. MCFARLAND: Good.

*(A long moment of profound mutual attraction. He kisses her on the forehead.)*

ELIZABETH: ... Doctor McFarland?

DR. MCFARLAND: Merely a kiss of charity, my dear.

ELIZABETH *(Confused, flushed)*: ... Thank you.

*(Pause.)*

DR. MCFARLAND: You must know, Mrs. Packard ... it is unusual to find a woman of such stimulating intelligence and learning in such a charming ... form.

*(Elizabeth laughs, blushes.)*

ELIZABETH: How nice of you to say so, Doctor.

DR. MCFARLAND: Your husband is . . . a . . . a fortunate man.

ELIZABETH: Early in my married life I learned the sad truth, Doctor. My husband does not . . . know me.

DR. MCFARLAND: Ah! I am sorry to hear it, Mrs. Packard.

ELIZABETH: . . . I was thinking just this morning . . . It's strange—I never knew my husband could do this to me. I wonder . . . if I'd known I would . . . *belong* to my husband . . . should I have married at all.

DR. MCFARLAND: Mrs. Packard! That would have been a—a calamitous choice for you to have made, I should think, a passionate woman like you!

ELIZABETH *(Flushes)*: . . . I . . . I could never, ever regret having my six beautiful children, don't misunderstand me, but . . . the price to pay is quite high, don't you think? I now better understand those women who choose not to marry. I could never understand them before! Or women who want to *vote*? I'm thinking *very* hard about them at the moment . . .

DR. MCFARLAND *(Horrified, but laughing)*: Good heavens! That is certainly not the cure I had hoped you would take away from this institution, Mrs. Packard! My dear, it is quite clear you're an exceptional woman . . . and if I were in the least bit unethical, I'm afraid I'd keep you here forever! I'd never want to let you out of my sight! *(Laughs; with irony)* But, sadly, I am a good man. *(They both laugh. She is uncertain. Pause)* Now . . . Let's use your prodigious mind . . . to find a solution to your dilemma, and I shall call that solution . . . a cure. *(Looks at her pointedly)* Do you understand me?

ELIZABETH: . . . I'm not sure . . .

DR. MCFARLAND: Well, then . . . Let's get to the heart of the matter, shall we? What is this about your saying you're . . . *(Finds it in his notes)* the personification of the Holy Ghost?

ELIZABETH: Wh-what? . . . I never said that. That would be . . . crazy!

DR. MCFARLAND *(With a smile)*: Yes . . . indeed. And it greatly concerns your husband that you did.

ELIZABETH: No, no! What I said—perhaps it isn't clear—is that the Trinity only makes sense to me if it consists of the Father, the Son, and the Holy Female Spirit. That is, the Son is the fruit of the love between the Father and the Holy Ghost. This idea has been discussed for centuries, Doctor.

DR. MCFARLAND *(Still with a smile)*: Really? And suppressed for centuries as heretical. Mrs. Packard, think! Your husband is a minister of the faith.

ELIZABETH: I don't care! It isn't heresy. The noun in Aramaic for Holy Spirit is *female*. It is a feminine noun.

DR. MCFARLAND *(Taken by surprise)*: . . . Really?

ELIZABETH *(Getting animated)*: Yes! And Jesus of Nazareth spoke Aramaic. Our good Lord Jesus Christ would not eliminate women from every possible interpretation of his Word. He assumed a knowledge of the language.

DR. MCFARLAND: Yes, well . . . *(Clearly fascinated)*

ELIZABETH: What may be of some confusion is I have said that, as a woman, I *represent* the female spirit in earthly form, just as you, as a man, represent the father and the son. You may not agree with this interpretation, but it is not delusional.

DR. MCFARLAND: Yes, well . . . it is even . . . quite interesting, Mrs. Packard. But you must be practical! What you have just said is irrelevant.

ELIZABETH: Irrelevant! Why?! . . . Why not discuss what is clearly interesting?

*(Pause.)*

DR. MCFARLAND: . . . If you and I were to have met under different circumstances, perhaps the two of us could indulge in . . . stimulating dialogue, but I am here to help you return home to your husband and children, posthaste. You must begin by promising me to keep these . . . thoughts to yourself.

ELIZABETH: No. I don't want to.

DR. MCFARLAND: Mrs. Packard, be reasonable! You must see that you cannot hold forth on these ideas in your husband's house.

ELIZABETH: But, Doctor, my children—

DR. MCFARLAND: No, no. Shh shh shh shh. I cannot be more clear. You have not given a response acceptable to your husband's teachings, and that must be our prime concern.

ELIZABETH: Then perhaps you should understand my husband's teachings, Doctor.

DR. MCFARLAND: No, no, you are here so I can understand you, Mrs. Packard, not your husband.

ELIZABETH: Then understand what I am up against, Doctor! My husband is not merely "a minister of the faith."

DR. MCFARLAND: How do you mean?

ELIZABETH: . . . My husband was a great sinner in his youth. *(Dr. McFarland: "Really? . . .")* He was a—a drunkard, and a wastrel and a disgrace to his minister father . . . *(Dr. McFarland: "Well . . .")* One night—hear me out—his little brother, Isaac, who was a sickly child, said to him: "Theo, have you looked after your soul?" . . . And Theo

had to answer no, he had not looked after his soul. Isaac
said: "Promise me you will *get right with God*, Theo." . . .
Those were his last words. Isaac died in Theo's arms.

DR. MCFARLAND: . . . I see . . .

ELIZABETH: Soon after, Theo had a vision and entered semi-
nary, reborn. *Do* you see, Doctor? My husband is
obsessed; he thinks only about damnation and is terrified
by any deviation from—

DR. MCFARLAND: Then do not deviate! Your task, Mrs.
Packard, is to accept your husband's beliefs and find a way
for you and your children to live within them.

ELIZABETH *(Suddenly wild-eyed)*: But, Doctor, a few months
ago, he said the children could not have *seconds* at supper!

DR. MCFARLAND *(Nonplussed)*: Pardon me?

ELIZABETH *(Beside herself)*: My husband locked himself away
for hours, praying for their souls, praying because they
wanted seconds!

DR. MCFARLAND: Mrs. Packard! What are you saying?

*(Pause.)*

ELIZABETH *(Snaps back)*: I have a mind—

DR. MCFARLAND: I know you have a mind, Mrs. Packard—

ELIZABETH: Well, I must use my mind.

*(Pause.)*

DR. MCFARLAND: Perhaps I should bring you paper and pen . . .
Mr. Packard says you like to write? . . .

ELIZABETH: Yes.

DR. MCFARLAND: I encourage you to write down your . . . very
interesting thoughts, and then perhaps you and I can dis-

cuss your musings . . . together, at length. I should like that. But what you write is not *ever* for your husband's eyes—that would only provoke him—only mine. Understood?

*(Elizabeth looks at him. A long moment.)*

I can be of great help to you, Mrs. Packard. I am sure of it . . .

*(He exits.*
*The lights change. Dr. J. W. Brown is on the witness stand. It is nighttime in the 7th Ward. Simultaneous scenes:)*

MR. HASLET: Doctor. Brown, did you make an evaluation of Mrs. Packard's mental state?

DR. J. W. BROWN: I did. I visited Mrs. Packard by request of Mr. Packard at their house three years ago . . . *(Pleased with his subterfuge)* She thought I was selling sewing machines. We discussed them at length. I found her completely rational on that subject. We spoke at length on women's issues, as well.

*(Mrs. Chapman and Mrs. Stockton enter to get ready for bed. Mrs. Bonner, resentfully leaves paper, pen and newspaper for Elizabeth.)*

We did not agree on those issues, but I did not think her *completely* insane on that subject. When we spoke of religion, however, I had no doubt that she was *hopelessly* insane and needed to be committed to the asylum.

*(Elizabeth, seeing paper and a pen on her bed, starts to write. Mrs. Chapman and Mrs. Stockton get ready for bed.)*

MR. HASLET: Can you give us your reasons, Doctor, for diagnosing her insane?

DR. J. W. BROWN: I can, sir. *(Takes out his notebook and reads from his notes)* If you don't mind I should like to read my reasons.

MR. HASLET: Go on.

DR. J. W. BROWN: Number one: *she disliked to be called insane.* Number two: she claimed perfection or nearer perfection in action and conduct than her husband! . . . Number three: she believed that to call her insane and abuse her was blasphemy against the Holy Ghost! Number four: she had an extreme aversion to the Calvinist doctrine of the total depravity of mankind and in the same conversation, she said her husband was a specimen of man's total depravity! Number five: she likened her marriage to the Civil War, saying she was the North and her husband was the South, and that man's despotism over his wife may yet now prevail, but she had right and truth on her side and ultimately she would prevail! Number six: she called me a rebel when I went out the door—a copperhead!—believed that some calamity would befall her owing to my being there, and took a great dislike to me. Number seven: she viewed the subject of religion from the *(Stumbling as he tries to read this)* esoteric standpoint of Christian ex . . . ex-eg-etical analysis, and—and ag . . . glut . . . inating the poly . . . syn—thetical ec . . . to-blasts of homo . . . geneous as—ceticism.

MR. HASLET: What? . . . Thank you, Doctor.

*(The lights change. The 7th Ward. An inmate whimpers behind the door. Concerned, Elizabeth goes to the door and tries to open it, but it is locked.)*

ELIZABETH: Hello! Hello! Who's there? Are you all right? *(No answer)* Are you all right? Do you need help?

*(Mrs. Bonner enters, runs to the woman, and starts to beat her. The women hear this from behind the door. The woman screams. More blows and groans. Mrs. Chapman and Mrs. Stockton sit up in bed.)*

Stop it! Stop it!
MRS. BONNER: Shut up, you!

*(Another blow and a groan. The other wards wake up. Cries and bellows.)*

ELIZABETH: Oh Dear God!
MRS. CHAPMAN *(To Elizabeth)*: Go to bed, dear. There is nothing you can do. Pray for sleep.

*(The Attendant enters and approaches Mrs. Bonner and the woman with a straitjacket.)*

MRS. BONNER: *QUIET Quiet! Or I'll knock you all to kingdom come! Quiet now!*
ELIZABETH *(Pounding on the door)*: Are you all right?!? Answer me!
MRS. BONNER: Jacket 'er.

*(Mrs. Bonner exits to the 8th Ward as the Attendant jackets the woman, then takes her off.)*

Quiet!! I'll skin yas alive! Qui-et!!!

*(Mrs. Stockton puts the pillow over her head and starts to cry. The bedlam builds to an ear-splitting madness, like a prison riot. Elizabeth prays, terrified. Blackout.*

*It is early the next morning. The lights slowly come up. Elizabeth has fallen asleep, fully dressed, pages of writing around her.)*

*(From off, as she enters)* All right, ladies. Get moving! Step lively! Special sewin' to do before breakfast.

*(Mrs. Bonner has a large basket filled with sewing and sewing boxes.)*

Let's go. Here y'are . . .

*(She distributes garments to the women as they wake up, exhausted, and throw on dresses. Elizabeth gathers her papers and gets herself ready.)*

Move along now, and make yer sewin' with yer very best hand, ladies. Yer mendin' for the doctor's family today . . . take care.

*(Elizabeth, surprised, looks at the others to see if they think her statement is unusual. Mrs. Bonner looks through the basket, finds something.)*

*(Pointedly)* Mrs. Packard, I have a skirt of Mrs. McFarland's for you to mend . . . there . . . right there, on the waistband.

*(Elizabeth takes the skirt. It is large. She meets Mrs. Bonner's eyes. A standoff.)*

ELIZABETH: Thank you.

*(As Mrs. Chapman sorts through the basket of clothes needing mending, Mrs. Stockton sits back down on her bed with a groan, exhausted.)*

MRS. BONNER: Mrs. Stockton! Get up off that bed, or I'll—

*(She palms her stick. Mrs. Stockton struggles up, terrified.)*

MRS. STOCKTON: Yes, yes! . . . I'm . . . sorry.

*(Mrs. Bonner exits, slamming the door. Silence.)*

*(Gathering herself)* At least we'll be doing something quiet and useful . . .

MRS. CHAPMAN: Yes, Mrs. Packard, take note. This is the sunny side of prison life.

*(Laughter.*
*Mrs. Chapman holds up each garment looking for where it needs mending. She passes a garment on to Mrs. Stockton. Wordlessly, the women look at the garments of what must be a large family of children. When Mrs. Chapman*

*holds up a sleeping gown for a fourteen–eighteen-month-old child, Elizabeth is stricken.)*

ELIZABETH: May I see that for a moment, Mrs. Chapman?

*(Mrs. Chapman hands it to her. Elizabeth looks at it, holds it, then brings it to her face, gets lost in it. The women watch, understanding. Suddenly aware, Elizabeth hands it back to Mrs. Chapman.)*

*(Quietly)* Thank you.

*(They sew. Finally:)*

MRS. CHAPMAN: What is your baby's name?
ELIZABETH: . . . Arthur . . . We have six children . . . *(To Mrs. Stockton)* And you?
MRS. STOCKTON: Blessedly, my children were already grown and on their own when I came here . . . They write to me . . .

*(They sew.)*

ELIZABETH: What happened last night?
MRS. CHAPMAN: . . . Someone was being disciplined for something or other, I should think. They call it "subduing the patient." It happens . . . many nights.
ELIZABETH: Really?
MRS. CHAPMAN: I hope it wasn't too bad for her.

*(They sew.)*

ELIZABETH: . . . I was wondering last night . . . Did you ladies know? Would you have done any differently—if you had known . . . the real consequences?

MRS. STOCKTON: That is a very good question, Mrs. Packard . . . Mrs. Chapman? . . .

MRS. CHAPMAN: Would I have done any differently . . . knowing I would end up here? *(After some reflection)* I don't know, but I think not . . . I think I would have done . . . just what I did . . .

ELIZABETH: Well . . . *(Pause. She wipes away quick tears)* I think the torment of being completely cut off from my children . . . I may not have been quite so outspoken, I think, if I had known the real cost.

MRS. STOCKTON: I tried to go home once . . . but I couldn't be quiet. I kept aggravating him, so I had to come back.

MRS. CHAPMAN: I never considered going home. *(Hatred just under the surface)* I wouldn't give my husband the pleasure . . .

*(They sew.)*

When I was young, I think I heard tales, sort of mutterings and rumors . . . But it did not seem to have anything to do with me somehow . . . I think I heard about wives thrown into madhouses—who knew where . . . Timbuktu!—but *vaguely*, we heard tell vaguely . . . on the wind almost . . .

MRS. STOCKTON *(Laughing)*: Yes . . .

*(They sew.)*

ELIZABETH *(A hard question)*: Do you ever wonder . . . if your husband is right?

MRS. STOCKTON *(Pointed)*: What do you mean?

ELIZABETH: I find myself doubting . . . myself—my very sanity, I suppose—deep down . . .

MRS. STOCKTON *(With force, taking her hand)*: You are sane, Elizabeth. Keep saying that to yourself over and over: "I am sane, I am sane." Let it become a little ditty in your head: "I am sane."

ELIZABETH *(Quiet, wiping away tears)*: Yes . . . Thank you, Mrs. Stockton.

MRS. CHAPMAN: Ladies . . . *(Speaks very softly looking to make sure no attendant is around)* I received a note from the 8th Ward yesterday . . . Mrs. Bonner beat a poor woman nearly to death during the night. She was in such a state, she . . . lost . . . consciousness while she was doing it . . . *(Gets up and holds Mrs. Stockton)* It was Mrs. Hosner, I'm afraid. *(Mrs. Stockton: "Oh Dear God." Handing the note to Mrs. Stockton from a secret pocket under her apron)* She hanged herself yesterday . . .

*(Mrs. Stockton is stricken.)*

ELIZABETH: What?

*(Dr. McFarland enters with Mrs. Bonner.)*

DR. MCFARLAND: Ladies . . .
WOMEN: Doctor . . .

*(Mrs. Stockton hides the note under her apron and tries to regain her composure.)*

ELIZABETH *(Helping cover for the women)*: Doctor McFarland! How nice to see you! I have just now finished mending your wife's skirt. It looks lovely, don't you think? *(She holds it up)* Now how does this work? Do I give you the bill for it now or later? *(He laughs)*

DR. MCFARLAND: Mrs. Packard, come over here and speak with me in private, please. Mrs. Bonner, you may clear the room.

MRS. BONNER: Come on, ladies. Off with you! And take yer sewin' with ya. Move along, Mrs. Stockton . . . Yer getting slower than molasses— *(A malicious warning in her ear)* Watch yerself.

*(Mrs. Stockton, upset, grabs Mrs. Chapman's arm as they leave.)*

DR. MCFARLAND: . . . Tell me, do you enjoy being provocative?

ELIZABETH: . . . Actually, I think I do. When it is warranted.

DR. MCFARLAND: Yes, I think you do, too.

ELIZABETH: I did not realize slave labor was part of the cure here at Jacksonville. *(He laughs)*

DR. MCFARLAND: Yes—your color comes into your cheeks when you are being provocative. It is very attractive.

ELIZABETH: Pardon me?

DR. MCFARLAND: Did you receive the paper and pen I left for you?

ELIZABETH: I did, thank you. I have already put them to good use.

DR. MCFARLAND: Excellent. I thought you might. So . . . Mrs. Packard—I assume you still want to leave Jacksonville . . . do you not?

ELIZABETH: Yes. Of course.

DR. MCFARLAND: As I told you, I shall miss you terribly, my dear, but I have decided not to be selfish. I shall let you go, painful as that is. In fact, you can elect to leave quite soon.

ELIZABETH *(Shocked, happy)*: Really? You're going to declare me sane.

DR. MCFARLAND: Mrs. Packard . . . I trust you have given our earlier discussion some serious thought?

ELIZABETH: Oh, yes . . .

DR. MCFARLAND: Good. I expected so. Then . . . I also expect you will submit to sign an affidavit to honor and obey your husband in all things—that you will be his unconditional help-mate and support in his church, in his home, and in his bed. Sign this paper, and I shall send you home, *cured.* Agreed?

*(Pause.)*

ELIZABETH: . . . Do you know what you are saying, Doctor?

DR. MCFARLAND: Oh, yes.

ELIZABETH: That if I submit to all my husband's wishes and opinions, I should be considered sane???! *(Laughs)* I should think it would mean just the opposite.

DR. MCFARLAND: Would you?

ELIZABETH: Yes! *(Getting angry, but remaining charming)* I will not ask you to put yourself in my shoes. Clearly, that would be asking too much, but let us say for just one moment that the tables were turned, shall we? *(Thinking on her feet)* Pretend for a moment you and I . . . were married . . . *(She holds his wife's skirt up to her; he laughs)* and we both teach at a school of great repute . . .

DR. MCFARLAND *(Amused)*: Yes . . . ?

ELIZABETH: You are beloved by students and faculty alike.

*(He is enjoying this.)*

DR. MCFARLAND: Go on.

ELIZABETH: I am not. In fact, I am feared and despised, and the students fall asleep whenever I lecture! *(They laugh)* Furthermore, you and I clash on simply every major issue facing the school. I decide to have you removed by force and committed to a lunatic asylum until you submit to me in writing that you will agree with me on every single issue we have previously clashed upon, even though during your confinement you realize you are further apart from my views than ever before. Would *you* sign? Would you find that situation acceptable? . . . Would you find my despotic behavior just? *(He laughs)* Or rather, would you not find me insane and fit for commitment to this asylum?

DR. MCFARLAND: You are quite a lovely woman . . . Dear God.

ELIZABETH: Doctor . . .

DR. MCFARLAND: Come, come, Mrs. Packard! What you just described is a fairy tale—a charming fairy tale—but a fairy tale nonetheless. What I am advising you to do is look clear-eyed at the world in which you have been placed, and save yourself, I beg of you.

*(Pause. A radical shift in tone.)*

ELIZABETH: . . . I sign . . . and I keep what I truly believe hidden from my children?

DR. MCFARLAND: Oh, yes. *Especially* from your children.

ELIZABETH *(Almost unable to speak)*: I don't know . . .

DR. MCFARLAND: Do you remember the healing treatment I gave you when you first arrived?

ELIZABETH: Yes, of course.

DR. MCFARLAND: Did it help?

ELIZABETH: Why, yes. Actually, I was able to sleep that night for the first time since I'd gotten here. I missed my children so much I couldn't bear it . . . I couldn't sleep . . . We all need to be touched, Doctor.

DR. MCFARLAND: Indeed . . . And it seems to me that you must get home to your children—if not your husband—as soon as you can. Do I understand your . . . desire? Or—?

ELIZABETH: No, you understand my desire.

DR. MCFARLAND: Good. However . . . I must admit, unlike you, I have not slept, Mrs. Packard . . . not since . . . *(He takes her hand)* You are a passionate and . . . beautiful woman. I marvel your husband can bear to be parted from you, even for a night.

*(Elizabeth laughs.)*

You cannot thrive here. Let me help you . . . Elizabeth. I would so enjoy . . .

*(They almost, almost kiss.)*

ELIZABETH *(A big decision)*: . . . Yes. I will . . . let you help me. My children need me. Wh-what do the papers say?

DR. MCFARLAND: What we have discussed, of course. That you will obey your husband . . .

ELIZABETH: Doctor . . . Why not let the papers say you release me . . . because I am sane?

DR. MCFARLAND: Madam?

ELIZABETH: You must not lie, Doctor; to lie is a sin.

DR. MCFARLAND: I do not—

ELIZABETH: Say: "Elizabeth Packard is not mad." Say: "Elizabeth Packard will not thrive here." Say: *(Intimate/*

*41*

*seductive)* "I will release you, Elizabeth, I will protect you, Elizabeth, I will deliver you . . ."

DR. MCFARLAND: Mrs. Packard . . .

*(They connect—a long, eroticized moment. Then he is the one to step back. A moment.)*

Perhaps I shall bring you the papers . . . to sign later today, or—or . . . in the morning . . . It's— best you leave as soon as possible.

ELIZABETH: Doctor—will you bring the papers—as presently written? . . .

DR. MCFARLAND: Yes, of course. *(With an edge)* There is no other way—to release you.

ELIZABETH: I see. You were not always as you are now, were you, Doctor? You had hoped for more, I'm sure.

DR. MCFARLAND *(Curt)*: . . . Good day, Mrs. Packard.

*(He exits, off balance.*
*The lights change. Dr. Christopher W. Knott is on the stand.)*

CLERK: Doctor Christopher W. Knott, you have been sworn.

DR. KNOTT: Sir, I have no doubt Mrs. Packard was insane. I would say that she was insane the same as I would say Henry Ward Beecher, Horace Greeley or the like are insane. Three-fourths of the religious community are insane in the same manner! Nothing excites the human mind quite so much as religion . . . Though Mrs. Packard is a lady of fine mental abilities, I observed she has a nervous temperament, is easily excited and has a strong will. Let us remember, gentlemen, the female mind is more excitable than the male mind. Confinement, in any shape, or restraint of any kind, I thought would only make Mrs. Packard's condition worse. Mrs. Packard required complete rest.

*(The lights change. That night. The women are in bed, trying to sleep. Silence. Then blows, a groan from off.)*

MRS. TENNEY *(From off)*: She can't breathe! Mrs. Bonner! Do you want to drown her?

MRS. BONNER: Ouchhh . . . All right . . .

*(Gasp. Choke.)*

It woulda been better if I'd killed her.

*(Elizabeth wakes up with a gasp.)*

MRS. CHAPMAN *(Firm)*: Mrs. Packard, pray for sleep.

MRS. BONNER *(From off)*: Yer useless!

ATTENDANT *(From off)*: Get back here!

*(The door bursts open. A woman in elegant attire, wild, wet hair, runs in, looking to get out, asking where "out" is. Mrs. Bonner enters, followed by the Attendant. Mrs. Bonner catches the woman and slaps her across the face. She grabs her and starts to drag her off.)*

ELIZABETH: Stop it! Stop it, Mrs. Bonner!

*(Mrs. Bonner stops and looks at Elizabeth—a dangerous moment.)*

MRS. BONNER: I am seekin' satisfaction and I will have it. I will not be abused by a patient. *(To the Attendant)* You! Take her back to the screen room and jacket 'er. She has the *divil* in her and I'm to beat it out of her.

*(The Attendant begins to take the woman off.)*

ELIZABETH: What has she done?

*(Mrs. Bonner exits, slamming and locking the door.)*

MRS. CHAPMAN: It doesn't matter, Elizabeth.
ELIZABETH: We have to do something.

*(Mrs. Chapman utters an odd laugh, then turns over trying to sleep. Elizabeth gets up, starts to throw on clothes. Mrs. Chapman sits up.)*

MRS. CHAPMAN: Elizabeth? What—?
ELIZABETH: The doctor's right—I have to get home to my children—
MRS. CHAPMAN: . . . Has he offered you the papers, dear?

*(A scream stops Elizabeth cold. She listens.)*

ELIZABETH: Oh dear God! I can't bear it anymore. I can't, I can't . . .

*(Elizabeth continues dressing.)*

*(To Mrs. Chapman)* Yes! I'll do anything . . . I'll sign anything . . . the children—

*(The scream becomes a screaming spasm, eerie in the still air. Elizabeth starts to cry, then stops herself. She makes a decision, races to her trunk, pulls out the writing paper.)*

MRS. CHAPMAN: Elizabeth, are you all right?
ELIZABETH: Yes, yes. Never mind, Mrs. Chapman. I'm sorry I've disturbed you . . . I—I . . . We can speak in the morning.

*(Elizabeth takes her pen and paper. She sits on the floor and starts to write. The wails continue.*
*The lights slowly change. Mrs. Dole is on the stand.)*

MR. HASLET: Was there a time you thought Mrs. Packard was unfit to care for her children?
MRS. DOLE: Yes. One day, Mr. Packard wanted me to take the baby, Arthur, home with me. Now Mrs. Packard consented, so I took the baby up to my house. In a short time, the other children came up and said their mother wanted to take her own child, so I took the child back down. Mrs. Packard's appearance was very wild, and she was filled with spite toward Mr. Packard. She called him a devil, and she defied me to take the child again, and said that she would evoke the strong arm of the law to help her keep it. Later that morning, they took her away. For the sake of the children, I approved of her removal.
MR. HASLET: Thank you.

*(The lights slowly shift. It is morning. The women are asleep. Elizabeth is still writing furiously. She has been writing all night. She blows out the candle as she hears Mrs. Bonner in the hallway, banging the doors with her stick and calling to the women.)*

MRS. BONNER: Step lively! Everyone up! Out of bed! Get on with you! . . . Step lively, ladies. Out of bed!

*(The women start to wake up. Mrs. Chapman sees Elizabeth sitting on the floor where she last saw her, still writing. She is ink-stained, looking wild and agitated, almost mad.)*

MRS. CHAPMAN: Mrs. Packard, have you slept?

ELIZABETH: No . . .

MRS. CHAPMAN: Mrs. Packard? Elizabeth! *(She goes to her)* What are you doing? My dear . . .

ELIZABETH *(Speaks quickly, manically)*: I am his favorite. I am writing him.

MRS. CHAPMAN: What? What do you mean? Whose favorite?

ELIZABETH: The doctor's! He . . . loves me.

MRS. CHAPMAN: Do not believe that, Elizabeth.

*(Mrs. Stockton approaches.)*

ELIZABETH: But he does! I will use my position for all of us. I'll not just help myself.

MRS. CHAPMAN: Elizabeth, what are you talking about?

ELIZABETH: There is no other way, Mrs. Chapman. I can appeal to the doctor's humanity and his good conscience— *(Mrs. Chapman laughs)* He will pronounce us *all sane* . . . And he will tell our husbands and our children we are sane. *(Mrs. Chapman: "No, he won't!")* He will change the . . . the degradation he fosters in this institution, or—or—

MRS. STOCKTON: Mrs. Packard! You must never tell a man like Doctor McFarland he is wrong.

MRS. CHAPMAN: He will punish you terribly for criticizing him, I fear, and then you will be of no use to yourself, your children, or any of us. I beg you, you have not had your sleep in weeks and you have written all night, pages and pages of—

ELIZABETH *(Out of control)*: Yes! This is my *reproof.* That is what I shall call it. *(She scribbles the title on the front page)* I shall tell him what is in it personally, and then I shall give him the pages to study so he and I can discuss it later, alone, at length, just as he promised—

MRS. STOCKTON: Mrs. Packard, wait. Get dressed and see him after breakfast. Your nerves are frayed now, my dear. You are exhausted and upset, and in no condition.

ELIZABETH *(Suddenly lucid and quiet)*: No! With all due respect, nothing will change if I stay here, as you two have. I have to do something. I will see him before breakfast if he is here.

MRS. CHAPMAN: Elizabeth! Sign the papers and go home.

ELIZABETH: *NO!!!!! I cannot go home on his terms!* I betray my children if I betray myself! I cannot go home and lie to them, pretending I agree with everything their father thinks and says and *believes*! *(Sobbing)* I can't do that to them! I can't do it! I can't!!

MRS. CHAPMAN: I understand, but you cannot do this.

*(Elizabeth breaks away. She goes to the door, calling:)*

ELIZABETH: Mrs. Bonner! Mrs. Bonner!

MRS. STOCKTON: What are you doing, child?

ELIZABETH: I cannot wait. If I wait, I might lose courage. Mrs. Bonner!

*(Mrs. Bonner comes to the door, her face bloated and bruised.)*

47

MRS. BONNER: What are you roarin' about?

ELIZABETH: I should like to speak with Doctor McFarland before breakfast please. Do you know if he is about?

MRS. BONNER: I seen him earlier.

*(Elizabeth moves to leave. Mrs. Bonner stops her with her stick.)*

You stay here. I'll see if *he* wants to speak to *you*. The rest of ya! Get dressed! Breakfast in five minutes! Step lively!

*(Elizabeth gets herself ready. She straightens her hair and buttons her dress. She collects her pages, putting half in the back of her mirror, which she returns to her trunk.)*

MRS. CHAPMAN: Elizabeth, I beg of you . . .

MRS. STOCKTON: This is suicide.

*(Elizabeth shakes her head.)*

ELIZABETH: No, this must be done, like Queen Esther in the Bible. She was the king's favorite, I—I . . . in case something happens to me—I have made a copy of the reproof. *(Mrs. Chapman: "What?!")* It is hidden in the back of the mirror. Remember that, will you? . . . He'll listen to me.

MRS. CHAPMAN: No, he will not!

ELIZABETH: I know him.

*(She starts to pace. Under her breath to herself, quickly:)*

"I am sane, I am sane." Make it a little ditty in my head: "I am sane . . ."

*(Dr. McFarland enters the room.)*

DR. MCFARLAND: Ladies?

WOMEN: Doctor . . .

DR. MCFARLAND: Mrs. Packard, you wished to see me?

ELIZABETH: Yes . . . Please.

MRS. CHAPMAN: We are going to breakfast, Elizabeth. *(As she leaves)* Shall we see you there?

*(Mrs. Bonner peeks her head in.)*

MRS. BONNER: Let's go then, ladies.

*(Mrs. Bonner looks at Dr. McFarland and Elizabeth suspiciously. After Mrs. Chapman and Mrs. Stockton leave, she closes the door.)*

ELIZABETH: Thank you for coming, Doctor.

DR. MCFARLAND *(Subdued, guarded)*: Pleasure. Now what can I do for you, Mrs. Packard? . . . Do you wish to sign your papers now?

ELIZABETH: Yes, perhaps I will sign them now, but first I want to give you the opportunity, to uh—I have been writing to you all night.

DR. MCFARLAND: Really?

ELIZABETH: Yes, Doctor. My heart feels as if it's bursting . . .

DR. MCFARLAND: Oh. Well, then . . .

ELIZABETH: I—I . . . I should like to read you some of what I wrote, or rather tell you in my own words what I am thinking and refer to my notes if I must—

DR. MCFARLAND: Of course.

ELIZABETH: And then give it to you to read so we can discuss it later, in depth—as you once proposed. *(Dr. McFarland: "Yes . . .")* As you can see, I wrote quite a lot to you—for your eyes only . . .

DR. MCFARLAND *(Laughs, relieved)*: Yes, I see. I look forward to our discussion . . . In depth, as you say.

ELIZABETH: I hope you will let me get to the very end since it is complex all I have to tell you.

DR. MCFARLAND *(Indulgent)*: Do . . . go on.

ELIZABETH *(Reading)*: "Dear Doctor McFarland, in Christ's own expressive language I say: 'Come let us reason together.'"

*(He smiles and sits.)*

DR. MCFARLAND: Please, continue.

*(She sits with him on the bed.)*

ELIZABETH *(Hesitates; then resumes reading)*: "Doctor, I would never dream of contradicting you or criticizing you in any way. You are the doctor, I the patient. But . . . there are things you may be ignorant of occurring in this institution th—"

DR. MCFARLAND: Pardon me? I must interrupt you. *(Laughing)* What do you think I could possibly be "ignorant of"?

ELIZABETH: Please, Doctor, let me just get the sense of this out. I am confident you will understand once I do.

DR. MCFARLAND: Perhaps we should discuss this at another time. You look upset this morning and not quite yourself.

ELIZABETH: No, no. Please, Doctor McFarland, please allow me to continue. I have not slept, that is true, but let me continue to—

*(A long pause.)*

DR. MCFARLAND: Yes?

ELIZABETH *(Reading)*: "I—I appeal to your great humanity, your power to heal, care for, and protect the sick and powerless in need ... You see—" *(She stops)*

DR. MCFARLAND: Mrs. Packard? ...

ELIZABETH: Your hands calm me, Doctor. May I ... take your hand? ...

DR. MCFARLAND: All right ...

ELIZABETH *(Taking his hand, steeling herself; reading)*: "Doctor ... it is my honest opinion ... that the principle upon which ... upon which—"

DR. MCFARLAND: Yes?

ELIZABETH *(Reading)*: "Upon which ... some of your staff ... treat ... some of the inmates of this institution is contrary to reason, to justice, and to humanity, and—"

DR. MCFARLAND: Wha—?! What did you say?

ELIZABETH: Please, Doctor. Hear me out— *(She continues reading)* "You are a renowned physician and a humane person. Perhaps you do not know what goes on here ..." *(Dr. McFarland: "Excuse me?")* "... but some of the patients are treated here in your institution in a very insane manner." *(Dr. McFarland: "Now wait—")* "No human being can be subjec—"

DR. MCFARLAND: Mrs. Packard! What are you saying? You of all people should know I—and my staff—are dedicated to healing and caring for those in mental torment. It is my life's work, Mrs. Packard. *(Elizabeth: "Of course.")* I thought you of all people truly understood (me) ... my position ... *(Elizabeth: "Yes ...")* and though I am well known for running a highly disciplined institution, this is essential for the well-being of the patients. *(Elizabeth: "I—I . . .")* Otherwise, there would be . . . mayhem, absolute chaos! And no patient could be treated.

ELIZABETH: Of course. Yes! I *do* understand, and that is why I must tell you—I hear the women through the walls. It is horrifying the trials they must endure. *(Dr. McFarland: "Mrs. Packard, clearly—")* Doctor, if you could hear them, if you could imagine for just one moment your own wife or your daughters going through the beatings these wives and daughters are put through— *(Dr. McFarland: "I—")* If you could picture that in your clear mind—I believe you would change the methods your staff uses to—to tend to the pa—

DR. MCFARLAND: That is quite enough!

*(Silence.)*

Mrs. Packard, I am one of the most respected doctors of the mentally ill in this country. My integrity is unimpeachable. Mentally ill patients are not mistreated under my watch, if that is what you are implying. Quite the contrary, as *you* should *well know*. I am sure you misunderstand what you hear.

ELIZABETH: Doctor, you are a loving and compassionate man. I understand you well, sir, just as you understand me—I felt your warm, healing hands. I know how you kissed me . . .

DR. MCFARLAND *(Overlapping)*: What are you . . . *(Stammering)* insinuating? —Wh—

ELIZABETH: And I beg of you!—release the sane inmates. *Declare* us sane. *(Dr. McFarland: "Mrs. Packard—")* Our children need us, Doctor. We have so much to contribute outside of this prison.

DR. MCFARLAND *(Outraged)*: Prison?! This is not a *prison*, Mrs. Packard! The women who are patients here must be kept here for their own health and protection and for the protection of their children.

ELIZABETH: No, Doctor. Look calmly at all you do that's good, but also admit that in my ward alone there are sane women who have been held here unjustly for years and years. *(Dr. McFarland: "That is un—")* You are not healing these women; you are merely doing our husbands' bidding. *(Dr. McFarland: "What?! How d—?")* Are you helping Mrs. Chapman, Doctor, or Mrs. Stockton? Are you?? *(Dr. McFarland: "You have no—")* As a sister in Christ, "Do unto others as you'd have them do unto you." I speak out of love and respect, in the hopes that you will . . . reform.

DR. MCFARLAND: What a grossly presumptuous statement.

*(She says nothing. A long pause.)*

I am extremely—angry . . . Mrs. Packard.

ELIZABETH: Yes.

*(Another long pause.)*

DR. MCFARLAND: I am an eminent man. A highly respected man. Do you not know that?

ELIZABETH: Yes, I know you are . . . And you want to be a good man. *(With profound emotion)* Do not turn your back on God. If you do, you'll die. You'll die by your own hand.

*(A long pause.)*

DR. MCFARLAND: —Good God, woman! What are you . . . saying—?

ELIZABETH *(Deeply felt, quiet)*: I know to love each other is impossible, Doctor. You are married before God, as am I, but you should know, I never gave my heart. It is whole and complete, and I give it now, to you.

*(He stares at her, haunted. Silence. They lose themselves in each other's gaze. Finally, he turns, goes to the door, and calls:)*

DR. MCFARLAND: Mrs. Bonner!

*(He turns back to Elizabeth.)*

ELIZABETH *(Relieved)*: Yes, Mrs. Bonner is one of the worst offenders.

*(Mrs. Bonner enters. She looks at Elizabeth, suspiciously.)*

MRS. BONNER: Doctor?

*(Startled, he turns to Mrs. Bonner.)*

DR. MCFARLAND *(Quietly, hoarse)*: . . . Please escort Mrs. Packard to the yard. She is in need of some air.

ELIZABETH: What? No . . .

*(Mrs. Bonner moves to take her. Elizabeth stands her ground.)*

No! Doctor!! Please . . . I heard her just last night—she said it would have been better if she'd *killed* the patient!

MRS. BONNER *(Under her breath)*: Shut yer mouth you. Just shut it.

ELIZABETH: . . . I heard you! I saw you Mrs. Bonner!

MRS. BONNER: She saw nuthin'.

*(Elizabeth moves to Dr. McFarland, imploring, pulling at him.)*

ELIZABETH: Doctor, I heard her! Don't you believe me? Doctor, please I beg of you.

DR. MCFARLAND: Quiet her.

*(He disengages from Elizabeth. Mrs. Bonner grabs her.)*

ELIZABETH: NO!!! . . . NO!! . . . I will not be *quiet*!! *(She struggles)* I will *never* be quiet!!!

MRS. BONNER *(Shouting to an Attendant, off)*: Callin' an attendant! Subdue the patient!

ELIZABETH: If you know what goes on here, Doctor, *you* are insane— *(Sobbing)*

*(Dr. McFarland wheels on her, enraged.)*

DR. MCFARLAND: What did you say?

*(The Attendant enters.)*

ELIZABETH: Insane!!—for knowingly inflicting pain on powerless people in need, and it warrants imprisonment . . . *for life* as you imprison others!

*(The Attendant throws Elizabeth to the ground. He shackles her.)*

I feel called of God and I shall obey his call to expose your character and the character of your institution unless you *repent*.

DR. MCFARLAND *(In real pain)*: You . . . you ungrateful—why are you doing this?

ELIZABETH: I have ability, I have God's promised aid—

DR. MCFARLAND *(Betrayed love)*: I gave you everything! Every possible—why are you questioning my . . . my integrity—my—

ELIZABETH *(Overlapping)*: I have friends who will help me . . . break the chains that bind us here—in—in slavery!

DR. MCFARLAND *(Overlapping)*: Quiet! Quiet her!

ELIZABETH: . . . Doctor, please . . . I am . . . your truest . . . friend . . .

*(Pause.)*

DR. MCFARLAND *(In turmoil, pain and rage)*: Mrs. Bonner, take Mrs. Packard upstairs to the 8th Ward. Treat her as you do the maniacs. Bring her belongings down to the trunk room. She is to have *nothing*.

*(As Mrs. Bonner drags Elizabeth off, Dr. McFarland picks up the pages and starts to read. The sound of a prison door clangs shut.)*

# ACT TWO

꧁꧂

*Minutes later.*

*The 8th Ward: bellowing, screaming mayhem; the ward is filled with maniacs. The floor is strewn with mattresses and refuse, the walls are covered in filth. The inmates are very dirty, not having been bathed in years, and they sit in their own excrement.*

*Elizabeth is pushed on by a jubilant Mrs. Bonner. The matron of the 8th Ward, Mrs. Tenney, approaches. She is a kind, timid, middle-aged woman.*

*Elizabeth can barely breathe from the stench.*

MRS. BONNER *(Happily)*: Welcome to yer new home, darlin'. *(Unlocks the shackles)* Mrs. Tenney, this is Mrs. Packard. She's a mad one. Dr. McFarland has removed her from the 7th Ward and wants you to admit her here where she belongs, in the 8th.

MRS. TENNEY: Thank you, Mrs. Bonner. Hello, Mrs. Packard.

*(Elizabeth nods.)*

57

MRS. BONNER: She's to have nuthin'. Nuthin' at all. Her belongings have been taken to the trunk room. Doctor's orders.

MRS. TENNEY: Is she violent?

MRS. BONNER *(With a malicious glint)*: Oh, she can be. Sometimes . . .

*(Elizabeth shakes her head. Her eyes meet Mrs. Tenney's.)*

ELIZABETH: How do you do, Mrs. Tenney.

MRS. TENNEY: Leave her with me, Mrs. Bonner. Thank you. I'll take care of her from here.

*(Mrs. Bonner exits. Elizabeth looks around her, tries to compose herself. After a moment:)*

Follow me please, Mrs. Packard.

*(The women pick up their skirts and step over the filth on the floor as they walk over to a bedstand covered with filthy rags. One of the inmates watches them, curious.)*

This will be your bed.

*(Elizabeth closes her eyes, almost dizzy.)*

ELIZABETH: I see . . . Are there . . . any clean sheets I could have?

MRS. TENNEY: Excuse me? I'm afraid not.

ELIZABETH *(Looking around)*: Is there a place to bathe? That is, if one knew how?

MRS. TENNEY: Oh, not really, no.

*(Pause.)*

ELIZABETH: It's practically impossible to breathe.

MRS. TENNEY: Once or twice a week some men come in and shovel it all out.

*(Long pause.)*

ELIZABETH: Like a barn.

MRS. TENNEY: Yes, like a barn.

*(Pause.)*

ELIZABETH: Do the doctors or the superintendent, then, not come here often, Mrs. Tenney?

MRS. TENNEY: Rarely, Mrs. Packard. They rarely come to the 8th Ward, if at all. I have never seen Doctor McFarland here.

ELIZABETH: I see.

*(She looks around; her survival instinct starts to kick in.)*

What is that bowl over there?

MRS. TENNEY: Oh, yes, that is a bed pan we thought to try on one of the less disturbed patients, but she wouldn't have it near her. So we are sending it back down.

ELIZABETH: Don't do that. It will make a splendid wash bowl. And show me where the facilities are located that *you* use. I should like to use them as well.

MRS. TENNEY: Pardon me?

ELIZABETH: That red ribbon—do you need it? I'm sorry to ask, but perhaps we could . . . tie it around the handle of the bed pan to make it clear to all the attendants that it is mine personally, all right? And they must not handle it. I'll keep it clean. Just show me where to rinse it. Now let us find me some soap and a towel, even a piece of toweling will do. I must bathe once a day, even if it is only a sponge bath. Is that true for you as well?

MRS. TENNEY: Why, yes, it is. I myself bathe daily . . . too. *(Giving her the ribbon)*

*(Elizabeth looks at her, expectantly.)*

Oh, yes. I will try to find you soap and a towel.

ELIZABETH: Don't try, Mrs. Tenney. Do it. I know you can.

MRS. TENNEY: Yes, yes I-I- will t— *(She stops herself)*

*(As Elizabeth ties the ribbon:)*

Have you angered the doctor, Mrs. Packard?

ELIZABETH: I have, Mrs. Tenney.

*(Elizabeth finishes tying the bow. She is exhausted, but discovers a kind of clarity.)*

You know, I am almost relieved to be here?

MRS. TENNEY: Excuse me?

ELIZABETH: At least it's clear now. Since I cannot tend my children—what the Lord would have me do.

*(She looks around. Silence. Then, she picks up the rags from off the "bed.")*

Can you find some buckets and soap . . . Let's boil these. *(Hands the rags to Mrs. Tenney)* In fact, let's strip all the beds, and then we must take all the rotted straw, throw it out and restuff these mattresses. *(Mrs. Tenney: "Wh—?")* They stink. Are there more attendants? *(She throws her mattress to the ground and opens it up)* Perhaps you and I can scrub and delouse the patients as well. *(She laughs)* Think of me as a colleague, why don't you? And by the way, I need someone to go to the trunk room and retrieve my mirror for me. It . . . means a great deal to me.

*(Mrs. Tenney, bewildered, watches Elizabeth work.)*

MRS. TENNEY: . . . Oh, oh . . . Why, yes . . . yes . . . of course . . . I—I—

*(Mrs. Tenney exits. Elizabeth continues to gut the mattresses and tend to the patients.*
    *Time passes. Dr. McFarland enters. She sees him but continues cleaning. He watches her, amazed she is cleaning the ward. After a while:)*

DR. MCFARLAND: Good day, Mrs. Packard.

*(After a long time, with contained fury:)*

ELIZABETH: Doctor, there is always something that can be done for the benefit of others, and since I hadn't the opportunity to do missionary work at home, I thank you for assigning me quite a large missionary field here to cultivate.

DR. MCFARLAND: Yes. Our good works are never enough, Mrs. Packard. We require grace. Did you learn nothing from your husband? . . . Or your father?

ELIZABETH: I should like some paper and a pen.

DR. MCFARLAND: You did forfeit that right.

*(She works.)*

ELIZABETH: Why are you here, Doctor? You never visit the 8th Ward, I understand.

DR. MCFARLAND: I wanted to . . . observe today . . . And see how you are . . . getting on.

ELIZABETH: Now you see.

DR. MCFARLAND: Yes.

*(She works.)*

ELIZABETH: Why are you still here?

*(No answer.)*

Would you like to talk now— *(With irony )* in depth? Or help me with the work?

DR. MCFARLAND: I am on my rounds. I have other duties and patients in need besides you, Mrs. Packard.

ELIZABETH: Indeed you have, Doctor . . . And yet you cannot stay away.

DR. MCFARLAND: Pardon me?

ELIZABETH: Tell me, Doctor, have you slept?

DR. MCFARLAND: No, I have not slept . . . I am too much awake.

ELIZABETH: I'm sorry. Perhaps your soul is not quiet.

*(Pause. He turns abruptly to go.)*

I will not see you again—at least not soon—will I?

DR. MCFARLAND: No. Perhaps not.

*(An inmate at the other end of the ward attacks another inmate. Bedlam ensues. Elizabeth calls for Mrs. Tenney. A male Attendant and Mrs. Bonner enter and separate the women, then the Attendant slugs the instigator in the mouth. She crumples to the floor, unconscious. The Attendant picks up the woman and carries her off like a sack.)*

*(Shaken, but covering)* . . . You see, Mrs. Packard—discipline is utterly necessary for the well-being of the patients.

ELIZABETH: Doctor! Surely you see this is an immense disgrace?

DR. MCFARLAND *(Heatedly, defending himself)*: Mrs. Packard! I do see the world for what it is . . . and I choose to *live* in it . . . Just as you should.

ELIZABETH: Ah. Yes. Well . . . I had thought better of you.

*(Pause.*
*Dr. McFarland exits. The door clangs shut behind him. The lights change. Miss Sarah Rumsey is on the stand.)*

MR. HASLET: State your name please for the record.

SARAH RUMSEY: Miss Sarah Rumsey.

MR. HASLET: How do you know Mrs. Packard?

SARAH RUMSEY: I worked for one week in Mrs. Packard's house as a favor to Mr. Packard. When Mrs. Packard found I was going to stay in the house and that the French servant had been discharged, she ordered me into the kitchen! Before that she had treated me kindly as a visitor. I thought it an evidence of insanity for her to order me into the kitchen. She ought to have known I was not an ordinary servant.

*(The lights change. In the 8th Ward, Mrs. Tenney gives Elizabeth paper from a hidden pocket in her apron. From a hiding place in the ward, Elizabeth retrieves pages of writing and gives them to Mrs. Tenney, who stashes them in her hidden pocket. Elizabeth writes a note, as Mrs. Tenney goes to tend a patient. Then she joins her.*
*The lights change.)*

MR. HASLET: Were you present at the interview when Mrs. Packard ordered the congregants from the church to leave the house?

SARAH RUMSEY: I was. Mrs. Packard was very pale and angry. She was in an undress and her hair was down over her face. It was eleven o'clock in the forenoon.

MR. HASLET: Did you stay at the house?

SARAH RUMSEY: I did. I stayed at the house. Mrs. Packard came out to the kitchen. She was dressed then. She said she had come to reveal to me what Mr. Packard was. She talked very rapidly; she would not talk calm. Said Mr. Packard was an arch deceiver; that he and members of the church had made a conspiracy to put her into the insane asylum. She wanted me to leave the conspirators. Said she had a new revelation, and that she had been chosen by God for a particular mission. She said that if I would side with her, I would be a chief apostle in the millennium.

MR. HASLET: Thank you, Miss Rumsey.

*(The lights change. The 8th Ward, months later. It is cleaner. Elizabeth and Mrs. Tenney wash a patient, the woman we saw earlier dressed so elegantly. Months of living in the 8th Ward have given Elizabeth a steely, hard-won strength.)*

MRS. BONNER *(From off)*: I'll do no more cleanin' up after yer kind! Whoo-hoo! Mrs. Tenney!

*(Mrs. Bonner enters, shoving on a crying Mrs. Stockton.)*

*(Delighted with her prey)* I got a lazy one here for isolation! Hands over your head!

*(Mrs. Bonner rips Mrs. Stockton's night gown off. Elizabeth looks up at her.)*

ELIZABETH: Mrs. Stockton?

MRS. STOCKTON *(Crying, muttering)*: Oh, Elizabeth, I shall die of shame . . .

ELIZABETH *(To Mrs. Bonner)*: How dare you?

MRS. BONNER: Come on with ya. That way.

*(As Mrs. Stockton turns to go, Mrs. Bonner smacks her on the rump. Mrs. Stockton, humiliated, runs naked toward the door. Mrs. Bonner laughs.)*

ELIZABETH: Stop it! Stop it! How da—?

*(Mrs. Tenney stops Elizabeth as Mrs. Bonner turns and glares at her—a dangerous moment. Then Mrs. Bonner exits, following Mrs. Stockton to the isolation room.)*

MRS. TENNEY: Don't try to stop her, dear. That would be dangerous for Mrs. Stockton. Look to your patient. I'll see after your friend.

*(Mrs. Tenney exits to look in on Mrs. Stockton. Sounds of Mrs. Stockton in distress are heard from off. The patient*

*Elizabeth is tending looks up and starts to chant in a little voice: "Peter, Peter, pumpkin eater, had a wife and—"*
  *Dr. McFarland enters in a fury, carrying a sheaf of papers. The ward erupts.)*

DR. MCFARLAND: Leave that patient.

*(Slowly and defiantly, Elizabeth continues washing the patient. More sounds of distress from Mrs. Stockton. The other inmates, alarmed, start to wail.)*

Mrs. Packard! Have I not repeatedly told you that you were not to have pen or paper?

*(Elizabeth calmly looks at him. She does not answer. Sounds from off of Mrs. Stockton choking on the water treatment.)*

Did I not? *(No answer)* Why have you been pretending you have nothing with which to write? *(Still no answer)* For months now, I have forbidden you to write. Why have you been lying, Mrs. Packard? *(Mocking her)* "To lie is a sin."

*(Elizabeth is about to answer. Instead, a silent standoff.)*

MRS. TENNEY *(As she reenters from the isolation room)*: She's had enough now, Mrs. Bonner. I'll get you a blanket, Mrs. Stockton.

*(We hear Mrs. Stockton whimpering, off.)*

DR. MCFARLAND: Ah, Mrs. Tenney! How did Mrs. Packard get paper and a writing utensil? Did you supply her with them?

*(Mrs. Tenney is about to answer yes. Elizabeth gets up to stuff a mattress.)*

ELIZABETH *(Icy calm)*: She did not.

DR. MCFARLAND: Mrs. Packard, I will ask you again: how did you get the paper and pen with which to write this document?

*(Before Mrs. Tenney can answer:)*

ELIZABETH *(Striving to stay quiet and steady)*: Doctor, do you not know that all of the inmates who have any wits about them, as well as much of your staff—except for Mrs. Tenney, of course—want to expose to the world both you and this abomination you call an asylum? They want to aid me in any way they can. They supply me with paper; they inform me about what is really happening inside this institution, and I write it all down.

*(Mrs. Bonner enters from the isolation room; we hear whimpers from Mrs. Stockton, off.)*

Can you hear that? That is Mrs. Stockton—a woman of seventy years and complete virtue—who is now in your isolation room—naked!—after undergoing a torture session from Mrs. Bonner.

DR. MCFARLAND: Mrs. Stockton needed disciplinary action, Mrs. Packard, and is completely safe.

ELIZABETH *(Facing him off)*: That's a lie. Are you going to straitjacket and gag the lot of us? You are losing this battle, Doctor. I warned you I would expose you.

*(Mrs. Tenney is terrified. Elizabeth goes back to stuffing mattresses. Whimpering from Mrs. Stockton continues to be heard from off.)*

DR. MCFARLAND *(With contained fury)*: It is unwise of you to declare war on me and my institution, Mrs. Packard. Mrs. Tenney, if I find in future that Mrs. Packard has the use of paper or pen, you will lose your position immediately.

MRS. TENNEY: Yes, Doctor.

DR. MCFARLAND: I don't care how hard it might be to replace you, but replace you I shall. Do you understand me?

MRS. TENNEY: Yes, Doctor.

DR. MCFARLAND: . . . You may go.

*(Mrs. Tenney nods. She finds a blanket and runs to the aid of Mrs. Stockton.)*

And Mrs. Packard, I shall replace Mrs. Tenney with someone who is not so sympathetic, nor soft, nor kind. Do you understand me? Someone will run this ward whose job it is to make you obey my rules! Mrs. Bonner, I thank you for bringing these . . . ravings to my attention.

*(Mrs. Bonner exits.)*

What you wrote here is libelous—lies! Mrs. Packard. Pages and pages and pages . . . all lies! This scribbling only confirms to me your complete and total madness! *(He starts to leave in a rage)* I should never again let you see the light of day.

ELIZABETH: Doctor, where are the letters from my family? A little bird tells me a pile of mail for me has sat on your desk for months.

*(He stops.)*

DR. MCFARLAND: You have no right to your mail.

ELIZABETH: No right? Why not? I am not a criminal. It cannot be legal for you to withhold my mail.

DR. MCFARLAND: It is perfectly legal. You are in the ward for the hopelessly insane. The inmates do not receive mail here.

*(She shakes her head, almost laughs.)*

ELIZABETH: Well . . . have you sent the letter I wrote to my husband?

DR. MCFARLAND: I will not send the letter you wrote to your husband. Not ever.

ELIZABETH: Why not?

DR. MCFARLAND: You have no right to set conditions to your husband for your release! Only I decide when and if to release you. You write to him he must repent!? *(Laughing)* You must be joking! Indeed not, my dear lady! *You* are the one to repent, not him and not . . . me. You daily prove to me that you are all that your husband represents you to be, that he is an abused man, a fine minister of the cloth, saddled with a . . . a defiant, trouble-making and profoundly disturbed wife who refuses the much needed treatment offered her to get well!

ELIZABETH *(Laughing)*: Oh, I see. Signing a document promising to lie was the "much needed treatment offered me to get well"!? Ah! *(Icy clear)* What is your master plan, Doctor? Can you tell me, or is it criminal? I have nearly been killed twice here in this ward by my "roommates" during the night. Is that what you and my husband want? To either make me into a maniac . . . or kill me?

DR. MCFARLAND: Mrs. Packard! You eschewed the special privileges I was more than willing to give you.

ELIZABETH: I did not!

DR. MCFARLAND *(With great force)*: *You most certainly did, madam!!* . . .

ELIZABETH: Oh . . . I see. I am terribly sorry if I hurt you, or . . . shamed you, Doctor. *(Honestly)* That was truly not my intent.

DR. MCFARLAND *(Explodes)*: You—you did not hurt me, Mrs. Packard, nor did you . . . *shame* me! I assure you! And that is completely . . . immaterial in any case. You belong here where I have put you, and you will obey *my rules* in this ward.

ELIZABETH: I see there is no way for me to get out of this institution while you are superintendent.

DR. MCFARLAND: I would be happy for you to be gone from this institution, believe me! You are nothing but an extreme annoyance to me. Worse, a howling fury who will not leave me in peace.

*(Elizabeth goes back to stuffing straw into the mattresses with great force.)*

ELIZABETH *(Quiet intensity, almost to bursting)*: Well, then, Doctor. Let my *husband* decide whether what he has done to me was right or not! Let him come here and see the hell-hole he has exiled me to. Let him stand in this room and see the maniacs . . . *(Trying not to scream at him)* and that I am NOT a MANIAC . . . and that neither he nor you can make me into a maniac!!! *(Dr. McFarland shakes his head; she tries not to cry)* Let him say how truly *sorry* he is that he threw his dear . . . wife . . . Elizabeth, into these horrifying . . . horrific . . . conditions! Let him admit that I was never deranged!! If he repents, I will return home to him!! I entered this institution *a sane woman* and I shall leave it as I entered it—a sane woman!! And for the sake of my children, you both shall CALL me SANE!

DR. MCFARLAND: Look at you. You're raving. I will state the obvious and this for the last time. Go home to your husband under the conditions I have outlined—in writing—or die here.

*(A pause. She breaks.)*

ELIZABETH *(Quiet, intimate)*: Doctor, my husband should be my protector, but he is not. Will you protect me? Please? . . . Will you be my husband in Heaven?

*(Elizabeth tries to embrace him, kiss him. He brutally disengages from her. Silence. Dr. McFarland stares at her, she at him.)*

DR. MCFARLAND *(Quietly)*: Why must you try to destroy every man who cares for you?

*(Dr. McFarland exits. Elizabeth reels, sits on the bed, begins to rock and cry.)*

ELIZABETH: Oh dear God, I'm going mad. *(She repeats this)*

*(The lights change. Abijah Dole on the witness stand, upset. Simultaneous scenes:)*

MR. HASLET: Mr. Dole, do you need a recess?

ELIZABETH: I am going mad . . .

ABIJAH DOLE *(Choked up)*: I—I'm fine thank you.

MR. HASLET: Mr. Dole, when did you know your sister-in-law was insane?

ABIJAH DOLE: I suppose . . . I knew she was insane the morning I found her in the west room still in her night clothes. It was almost noon! She took my hand and led me to the bed. The daughter, Libby, was lying in bed of brain fever. Mrs. Packard's hair was disheveled. Her face looked wild.

ELIZABETH: I'm going mad . . .

ABIJAH DOLE: The child was moaning and moving her head from side to side. I wondered if she had made the child deranged.

MR. HASLET: Did you see her soon after that at church?

ABIJAH DOLE: I did. I was then still superintendent of the Sabbath school. Just at the close of school—I was behind the desk—she appeared before me almost like a vision, and told me she pitied me for marrying my wife, who is a sister to Mr. Packard. She said I might find a more agreeable companion! She said that if she had cultivated amorousness, she would have made a more agreeable companion. She then requested to read or deliver an address to the Bible class.

*(Mrs. Tenney enters and places a cool cloth on Elizabeth's forehead.)*

MR. HASLET: How did she look?

ABIJAH DOLE: Very wild and excited. I did not know what to do. I knew Mr. Packard thought her insane and did not want her to discuss these kinds of things in the Sabbath school, but I did not want to take the responsibility myself so I put it to a vote. I was much surprised when the class allowed that she could read it.

MR. HASLET: What was the content of her address?

ABIJAH DOLE: I cannot recall, but it was evidence of her insanity. *(Starts to sob)* I knew she was mad.

*(The lights change.)*

ELIZABETH: I am sorry to put your position in jeopardy, Mrs. Tenney.

MRS. TENNEY: There, there . . . just breathe deeply now. It's my choice. I am glad to do it.

ELIZABETH: . . . For the sake of my children—I must not go mad . . .

MRS. TENNEY: That's right, Mrs. Packard.

*(After calming Elizabeth, Mrs. Tenney looks around to make sure no one is watching, then she pulls some papers from a pocket underneath her apron.)*

Here are testimonies from the ladies in the Fifth Ward. Shall I hide them in your bonnet, Mrs. Packard?

ELIZABETH: Please.

MRS. TENNEY: I've had your trunk brought up so we ladies don't have to sneak down to the trunk room anymore.

ELIZABETH *(With a half smile)*: You've defied the doctor, Mrs. Tenney? . . .

MRS. TENNEY *(Proudly)*: I suppose I have, Mrs. Packard.

*(Mrs. Tenney uncovers the trunk, which has been under a pile of sheets. She takes the pieces of paper and hides them in the lining of the trunk and in Elizabeth's bonnet.)*

ELIZABETH: Will you sit with me?

MRS. TENNEY: Why, of course. I forget you are a patient, and that you need care, as well.

ELIZABETH: It's not that I need care, Mrs. Tenney. It is that I am so terribly lonely. I always had my children to speak to at home . . .

MRS. TENNEY: I understand.

ELIZABETH: Until just weeks before he sent me away, my husband left the children entirely to me. I was always with them . . . Mr. Packard knows *nothing* about the children. That's why I'm so frightened for them. *(She wipes away tears)* He worried only about the children's souls. For some reason, he was afraid our little Isaac had been born damned. He'd go into his study for hours on end to pray for him and terrified the children with his constant talk of hellfire and everlasting torment.

*(Mrs. Tenney: "Tsk, tsk . . . shame . . ." Mrs. Tenney folds more papers into the bonnet.)*

I hated to bring up the children in fear, but I raised the children to honor their father, so—

MRS. TENNEY: Of course . . . *(They work)* Well, at least you hadn't a husband like mine.

ELIZABETH: How do you mean?

MRS. TENNEY: Well . . . mine just jumped into that bottle, and no one could get him out of it.

ELIZABETH: Oh, no . . .

MRS. TENNEY: Oh, yes . . . *(They work)* Why did you marry yours, dear?

ELIZABETH: I suppose I thought I loved him. I barely knew him. *(Mrs. Tenney nods: "Mmm . . . hmmm.")* I was a young bride, and he was very much older than I. Mr. Packard was a colleague of my father's, and *my* father respected *his* father, so it seemed an auspicious match. *(Mrs. Tenney: "Surely.")* I worshipped Mr. Packard's piety, I think. *(Mrs. Tenney: "Hmph.")* I wanted to be just like my mother—the wife of a beloved minister, mother of a large brood of children, and I was happy for a time. Mr. Packard was not beloved by any of his congregations, however—and though I loved motherhood, he was never really a natural husband . . . or father. I don't think I'd be in prison here today if I had married *anyone* else . . .

MRS. TENNEY: Well, don't blame yourself, dear. Lots of women marry the wrong man. I suppose I did, too, but at least I hardly knew mine. He died, very young . . .

ELIZABETH: I'm so sorry.

MRS. TENNEY *(Shrugs)*: Oh, perhaps it's a blessing.

*(The inmates become agitated as Mrs. Bonner enters the 8th Ward with an Attendant and a straitjacket. Mrs. Tenney quickly hides the papers, leaving the bonnet on the bed.)*

MRS. BONNER: All right, Mrs. Packard. No more naughtiness for you, my dear. It's off to isolation with ya.

ELIZABETH: What?

MRS. BONNER *(To the Attendant)*: Jacket.

ELIZABETH: What are you doing?

*(Elizabeth fights them off.)*

MRS. TENNEY: What are you doing to her?!

MRS. BONNER: She's to be in the isolation room three days. *(Crowing)* No more writin' for you, Mrs. Packard! Doctor McFarland's orders.

MRS. TENNEY: I don't believe Doctor McFarland would do that to Mrs. Packard.

MRS. BONNER *(Viciously turns on her)*: Oh, no? Go and ask him yerself.

MRS. TENNEY: I shall go to the doctor, Mrs. Packard. I will try to get you out.

*(She exits.)*

MRS. BONNER: Don't struggle, Mrs. Packard. It will hurt ya a whole lot more if ya do.

*(They finish straitjacketing Elizabeth and drag her off. The back wall opens to reveal the isolation room. Mrs. Bonner shoves Elizabeth inside. Mrs. Stockton is huddled in a corner, a blanket around her, muttering and crying. Elizabeth runs to her.)*

ELIZABETH: It's all right, Mrs. Stockton. Remember, "I am sane, I am sane." Keep your little ditty in your head—"I am sane."

MRS. BONNER *(Grabbing Elizabeth)*: I've looked forward to this moment for a long time, Mrs. Packard.

ELIZABETH: I'm certain you have, Mrs. Bonner.

*(Mrs. Bonner holds Elizabeth down in a tub of cold water and then brings her back up, gasping and coughing.*
*Dr. McFarland enters the 8th Ward and listens to Elizabeth's punishment.)*

MRS. BONNER: How are ya feeling now, Mrs. Packard?

*(Elizabeth does not answer.)*

Ochh. You won't say? I see. Well, you have to tell me when to stop, you know. Otherwise I won't. I won't stop.

*(Mrs. Bonner dunks Elizabeth again.*
*Dr. McFarland goes to Elizabeth's bed, rips off the bed-clothes, looking for papers.*
*The lights change. Mr. La Brie is on the stand.)*

MR. LA BRIE: I am the Justice of the Peace.

*(Dr. McFarland picks up the bonnet, puts it down.)*

I live fifteen rods from the Packard house.

*(Mrs. Bonner pulls Elizabeth's head up from the water.)*

I saw Mrs. Packard nearly every day—sometimes two or three times a day.

*(Mrs. Bonner dunks Elizabeth.)*

I have seen nothing in the six years I have known her that could make me think her insane. I am not a physician and I am not an expert, but if she be insane, no common sense man could find it out.

*(Mrs. Bonner pulls Elizabeth up brutally. She is practically unconscious.*

*Frustrated by his fruitless search, Dr. McFarland enters the isolation room. Elizabeth sees him. They lock eyes.)*

DR. MCFARLAND: Mrs. Bonner you may go.

*(Mrs. Bonner exits. Dr. McFarland pulls Elizabeth to her feet.)*

MR. LA BRIE: Of course, we all knew Mr. and Mrs. Packard were having difficulties. It was becoming public knowledge.

*(The lights change. Elizabeth clings to Dr. McFarland, sobbing. He holds her tight. A long embrace. Mrs. Tenney enters and sees them. Dr. McFarland quickly covers.)*

DR. MCFARLAND: Take Mrs. Packard to her bed, Mrs. Tenney.

*(Mrs. Tenney nods. She takes Elizabeth and helps her off.*

*Profoundly disturbed, Dr. McFarland stares at his reflection in the water. A moment of self-revelation.*

*The lights slowly change. The walls of the isolation room close as the lights come up on the 8th Ward, weeks later.*

*Elizabeth is very weak and depressed. She lies on her bed in a fetal position. Mrs. Tenney covers her with a blanket.)*

*Theophilus enters. The inmates see him and become agi-
tated, some start screaming. Elizabeth sees him and turns
away.)*

MRS. TENNEY: May I help you, sir? Visitors are not allowed on
this ward.

THEOPHILUS: I am Reverend Packard. That is my wife, Elizabeth. Doctor McFarland said I could come up.

MRS. TENNEY *(Surprised)*: Did he, really?

ELIZABETH *(Depressed)*: Mrs. Tenney, tell him to observe
where he's exiled his wife . . .

*(Mrs. Tenney does not know what to say.)*

THEOPHILUS: . . . I know you may not wish to speak with me,
Wife, but I must ask you some questions.

*(The patients become more and more agitated. Theophilus
is scared but tries not to show it.)*

*(To Mrs. Tenney)* Can you possibly stop their . . . howling?

MRS. TENNEY: I shall try, sir.

THEOPHILUS: Mrs. Packard, I have brought you some warm
clothing . . . *(Waits for her to thank him. She doesn't)* I have
brought you . . . greetings from the children. *(Elizabeth:
"Ah!")* Elizabeth, I have lost my position at the church.
I have lost my congregation. We have no money. We are
living on the handouts of former parishioners. I cannot
afford to keep all the children with me, and I am moving
back to Massachusetts. I am asking your advice on where
each child should go . . . The littlest ones can stay with my

sister. Toffy and Samuel can be on their own. That leaves Isaac and Libby. Libby is not well. She takes after your mother. She cries and weeps all day. I don't know what to do with her.

ELIZABETH: Oh dear God, Theophilus . . . What have you done to the children?

THEOPHILUS *(A broken man)*: What have I done?? Wife, your . . . illness has ruined us.

ELIZABETH *(Shakes her head)*: Have you seen the letter I wrote you?

THEOPHILUS: I have received no letters from you.

*(Long pause.)*

ELIZABETH: Nor I from you . . . or the children.

*(Pause.)*

THEOPHILUS: What was in the letter?

ELIZABETH: If you repent, I will come home. And *I* will care for the children.

THEOPHILUS *(Bewildered)*: Repent?

ELIZABETH: Oh, Theophilus. I once did care for you. And you for me. Admit sending me here was wrong. Ask my forgiveness and we will try again. I will try to forgive you.

THEOPHILUS: That is impossible. I cannot allow you near the children.

ELIZABETH: And why is that exactly?

THEOPHILUS *(Tears in his eyes; he explodes)*: *You know why!*

*(The inmates start to get upset. Mrs. Tenney calms them.)*

Here. *(He puts his bundles down on the bed)* I am leaving you some warm clothes and some writing paper. I know how much you like to write.

*(She almost thanks him. Long pause. He tries to answer her question:)*

God forgive me, Elizabeth . . . you frighten me . . . so very much. *(He sits)*

ELIZABETH *(Sad)*: I know, dear. *(She puts her arm around him)* . . . And I know you are quite certain what you believe is right, but there are many people, many intelligent people, who think you are wrong. I am merely one of them.

THEOPHILUS: Have you no advice for me about the children?

ELIZABETH: You will not take my advice. Please tell the children their mother loves them, to never doubt how much she loves them.

*(She gets up and pulls out sewing from her trunk. She pulls out letters sewn inside the garments.)*

Perhaps you will deliver these to the children. I will not have to smuggle them out if you do. And please ask the doctor to mail my letters in future. I know you have asked him not to and that I am to receive none. And I have not. I have received not one letter from family or friends since I arrived here . . . I suppose you poisoned my dear father against me, too, didn't you?

THEOPHILUS: Your father understands you belong in the asylum, Elizabeth. He was the one who committed you the first time.

ELIZABETH: He was mistaken to commit me! He thought it was a hospital he was sending me to. He admitted this to me years ago.

THEOPHILUS: Really? Well, not to me. In fact, quite the contrary, I'm afraid.

ELIZABETH: What? What do you mean?

THEOPHILUS: He told me only recently he believes he was right to have committed you when you were young.

ELIZABETH: Wh—? I don't believe you!

THEOPHILUS: He was going to write you, but when I told him what you had done, he agreed with me. You belong here, Elizabeth.

*(She is devastated. Pause.)*

ELIZABETH: Have you asked the doctor about . . . my progress, Theophilus?

THEOPHILUS: Yes . . .

ELIZABETH: He says I have worsened, has he not?

THEOPHILUS: I do not wish to upset you further, Elizabeth.

ELIZABETH *(One last try)*: Look around you, Theophilus! That's all I ask of you. Do I in any way resemble these poor women? *You* decide.

THEOPHILUS: Elizabeth, if you could only see yourself . . .

ELIZABETH: I am your wife. Take me *home*! *(She goes to him, embraces him)*

THEOPHILUS: I-I— *(He is deeply upset)*

*(Dr. McFarland enters. Elizabeth manages to hide some of the writing paper under her blanket.)*

DR. MCFARLAND: Reverend Packard—there you are!

THEOPHILUS: Doctor—

DR. MCFARLAND: Where did you get that paper, Mrs. Packard?

ELIZABETH: Mr. Packard gave it to me. I am sure he thought it an innocent amusement for me to write here, knowing I loved to write when I was at home.

DR. MCFARLAND: Let me see it.

*(She hands it to him.)*

I will take care of this. Reverend Packard, why did you give paper to your wife?

THEOPHILUS: As Elizabeth said, for her comfort and amusement.

DR. MCFARLAND: You must not do that. *(He swallows his rage)* If you ever attempt to interfere again with my management and discipline of your wife, you shall have the liberty of taking her away, forthwith. Do you wish to do that? Do you wish to take her away with you now?

*(A terrible silence. Will Theophilus take her home? A long moment. Dr. McFarland and Elizabeth watch him. Then Theophilus submits, silently.)*

Come with me, sir. You should not be here.

*(The men exit. Elizabeth collapses on the bed. Mrs. Tenney approaches.)*

MRS. TENNEY: I overheard, of course . . . *(Long pause) Lie!* Mrs. Packard, just lie. Women have been doing it since the beginning of time . . .

ELIZABETH *(Depressed)*: But . . . *I* can't . . . do it . . . And you
heard him—he'll never let me near the children again . . .
I've lost them . . .

*(She curls into a fetal position.)*

MRS. TENNEY *(Tough)*: Do not lie down in that bed. Come on,
up with you.

ELIZABETH: What? I cannot. I cannot just now, Mrs. Tenney.

MRS. TENNEY *(Tough caring)*: Then I shall help you. Come
on . . .

ELIZABETH: Please, just let me stay here a little while longer.
I am so . . . tired. *(She throws her arm over her head)*

MRS. TENNEY: I've seen it too often, Mrs. Packard. A patient
wants to stay in bed for a little while and then another little while, and then after a while she never gets out of bed.

ELIZABETH: What's the difference? Perhaps Mr. Packard and
Papa are right about me. I don't really care anymore, Mrs.
Tenney.

MRS. TENNEY *(With urgency)*: Well, I *do* care, Mrs. Packard!
Come on. Up with you! If you remain in this bed, you will
die in this bed. I have seen it before. Come on, up you
go . . .

*(Mrs. Tenney gets her up with difficulty as:*
*The lights change. A distinguished man with a Scottish*
*accent is on the stand.)*

DR. DUNCANSON: I am Doctor Robert Duncanson. I have
earned advanced degrees in both theology and medicine
from the University of Glasgow and Anderson University.
Mrs. Packard's explanation of woman representing the

Holy Ghost, and man representing the male attributes of the Father, and that the Son is the fruit of the Father and the Holy Ghost is a very ancient theological dogma, sir, and entertained by many of our most eminent and learned men. *(Laughs)* It is by no means a mark of lunacy.

*(The lights change. Music. The Lunatics Ball, six months later. Mrs. Chapman and Mrs. Stockton enter with Mrs. Bonner. They sit. The women from the 8th Ward are dancing. Simultaneous scenes:)*

I spoke with her three hours. With every topic I introduced, she was perfectly familiar and discussed them with an intelligence that at once showed she was possessed of a good education and a strong, vigorous and healthy mind.

*(Elizabeth enters, pale and depressed, shaky. She is escorted by Mrs. Tenney. She sees Mrs. Chapman and crosses to her.)*

I did not agree with all of her thoughts, but I do not call people insane because they differ from me, nor even from a majority of people.

ELIZABETH *(Very subdued)*: Mrs. Chapman, how good to see you. *(They hold hands)*

DR. DUNCANSON: You might as well with as much propriety call Galileo mad, or Newton, or Jesus, or Luther, or Morse who electrified the world!

MRS. CHAPMAN: We hear you are having a difficult time, dear.

ELIZABETH: Some days are better than others, but Mrs. Tenney helps me a good deal. She insisted I come to the ball tonight. *(They laugh)*

DR. DUNCANSON: With Mrs. Packard, there is lacking every indication of insanity that is laid down in the books. I pronounce her a *sane* woman, and wish we had a *nation* of such women.

*(The lights change.)*

ELIZABETH *(Conspiratorial)*: I'm not supposed to leave the 8th Ward. Doctor McFarland's orders.

MRS. CHAPMAN *(Looks at her piercingly)*: Oh, Elizabeth. Promise me you will not end up like our dear Mrs. Stockton.

ELIZABETH: What do you mean? *(Just now notices Mrs. Stockton)* Mrs. Stockton, how good to see you.

*(No answer. Mrs. Stockton looks blankly ahead.)*

Mrs. Stockton?

MRS. CHAPMAN: She has not spoken a word since she came back from the isolation room months ago.

ELIZABETH: . . . Oh, no . . . NO! . . .

*(Elizabeth kneels down in front of her and tries to look into her eyes.)*

Mrs. Stockton? . . . Hello, dear . . . Mrs. Stockton!?

*(Mrs. Stockton sits there. Tears stream down her cheeks, but she looks vacantly ahead. Elizabeth sees that Mrs. Stockton has lost the battle; her mind is gone.)*

. . . I'm so sorry, dear.

*(Elizabeth buries her head in Mrs. Stockton's lap.)*

MRS. CHAPMAN: Elizabeth, no crying now. *(Seeing Mrs. Bonner; bitter)* Do not give that woman the pleasure.

*(Mrs. Chapman and Mrs. Bonner meet eyes. Dr. McFarland enters, leading a group of prosperous-looking men: the asylum's trustees. He is giving a tour. Mrs. Chapman and Mrs. Tenney see him and shield Elizabeth from the doctor's sight.)*

DR. MCFARLAND: The Lunatics Ball is held twice a year in this auditorium. It is a welcome break from our institutional routine. Even some of the local townspeople enjoy coming!

*(Two of the dancing inmates start a fight.)*

MRS. BONNER: Stop that now, ladies! Stop it! Behave yerselves! *(Shoos them away)*

*(Dr. McFarland brings the trustees into the ball as one inmate starts to sing "The Battle Hymn of the Republic." Dr. McFarland stops the trustees near Mrs. Chapman's group. He doesn't notice Elizabeth.)*

DR. MCFARLAND: Gentlemen, perhaps you have met Mrs. Tenney. And this is Mrs. Chapman from our 7th Ward. Our best ward. Mrs. Chapman, some of our trustees!
MRS. CHAPMAN: How do you do?
DR. MCFARLAND: This way, gentlemen—

*(The men smile and nod and start to move on. Elizabeth sees her last chance and quickly extends her hand to the man who looks like he is in charge.)*

ELIZABETH *(Highly adrenalized)*: How do you do? I am Elizabeth Packard from the 8th Ward. *(Dr. McFarland: "Gentlemen, shall we—?")* The ward for the violent and hopelessly insane. I have been working since my incarceration there to clean it and clean the inmates and make a healing atmosphere for treating the sick. I do so hope you can see it on your visit.

MR. BLACKMAN: Really? . . . How extraordinary. I am chairman of the board, and I have never seen that ward.

ELIZABETH: Oh, then you must come. It has been transformed.

MR. BLACKMAN: Yes . . . Did you say you worked here, Mrs.—?

DR. MCFARLAND: Yes, Mrs. Packard has been a very helpful patient during her cure.

ELIZABETH: Yes, you see, I am actually *still sane*—and I do hope you will give me just ten minutes of your time so I may demonstrate my sanity to you.

MR. BLACKMAN: Well . . . You certainly are a charming and articulate creature, Mrs. Packard. I should think we could arrange . . . ten minutes. Doctor?

DR. MCFARLAND: . . . Mrs. Packard has been placed in the proper ward for her treatment and should not be disturbed.

MR. BLACKMAN *(A man used to running things and getting his way)*: Nonsense. Ten minutes would be fine, I should think . . . Tomorrow morning, after breakfast, Mrs. Packard?

DR. MCFARLAND: Mr. Blackman, I really must insist—

MR. BLACKMAN: In your office, Doctor? I look forward to it.

DR. MCFARLAND *(Angry, does his best to cover)*: Yes, of course, come this way, gentlemen. Good evening, ladies. Mrs. Packard.

*(As the trustees move on, Elizabeth meets eyes with Dr. McFarland, then he exits. The ball continues.*
  *The lights slowly change. Mr. Blessing is on the stand.)*

MR. BLESSING: I am Mr. William Blessing. My wife and I live eighty rods from the Packard house. I have known Mrs. Packard since she moved to Manteno. She visited at my house often. She attended the Methodist church for a while after the difficulties commenced, and then I saw her every Sunday. I never thought her insane. After the word was given out by her husband that she was insane, she claimed my particular protection. I thought her husband was insane if anyone was. I—I regret . . . I assured Mrs. Packard her husband could not commit her to a lunatic asylum without first proving her insane in a court of law. The morning I looked out my window and saw the men carry Mrs. Packard out of her house, I ran across the street to try to stop them. The sheriff informed me that Mr. Packard had every right to do what he was doing and I had better step back. Later, we tried to visit her at Jacksonville. I even wrote to the governor, but I learned there was nothing we could do to help her.

*(The lights change. The next morning, Dr. McFarland's office, low light. The trustees and Theophilus gather inside the office. Dr. McFarland waits for Elizabeth outside, nervous, pacing. Elizabeth enters, her arm gripped by Mrs. Bonner.)*

MRS. BONNER: Move quickly, Mrs. Packard, or ye'll be losing yer time . . .

*(Dr. McFarland greets them.)*

DR. MCFARLAND: Mrs. Packard! Ready for the meeting? I should like to escort you in myself.

*(She stops.)*

ELIZABETH: Would you?

DR. MCFARLAND: I think it would be a nicer entrance than if you were to enter on Mrs. Bonner's arm, don't you?

ELIZABETH: . . . Perhaps.

DR. MCFARLAND *(Pulling her close, conspiratorially)*: I trust you're going to take a good whack at Calvinism, Mrs. Packard—explicate your more *radical* views to the trustees?

ELIZABETH: Surely, you know I am.

*(Dr. McFarland guides Elizabeth into the office. The men rise. The lights brighten. Elizabeth, not having slept, nervous, strives for control.)*

MR. BLACKMAN: Good morning, Mrs. Packard.

ELIZABETH *(Charming)*: Good morning. Gentlemen, *(Cold, surprised to see Theophilus)* Mr. Packard . . . Thank you for agreeing to meet with me today. I know you are busy men, and I shall not go past my time.

MR. BLACKMAN: Please, have a seat.

ELIZABETH: Thank you, sir. *(She sits, nervous, suspicious of Theophilus's presence; a deep breath)* I am the wife of . . . Reverend Theophilus Packard, invited here today, I assume, by . . . Dr. McFarland?

DR. MCFARLAND: Indeed . . .

THEOPHILUS: That's right.

DR. MCFARLAND: Yes.

ELIZABETH: Let me begin by saying my husband would have me incarcerated here because I . . . do not believe any longer in his old . . . (to my mind), his *perversely* old-school Calvinist teachings. As the scales of bigotry have fallen from my eyes, gentlemen, I have found a great deal of truth and—and wisdom in other faiths—the Methodists, the Universalists, and even the Cath—

MR. BLACKMAN: I see, yes . . . however, I must warn you, Mrs. Packard, we are all Presbyterian. Some of us devout Calvinists from the old school, like your husband.

ELIZABETH: I . . . thank you for your warning, sir. *(She looks at Dr. McFarland)* However, I still beg you to listen to my thoughts . . . Though I may have differing beliefs from you or my husband, I hope you will see . . . I am not insane. *(Holding on to her fury)* Doctor McFarland thinks his charge is to keep me here until I am quiet and docile and accept all that my husband believes. Since I cannot ever believe again in what I consider to be my husband's narrow views of Christ *(Suddenly mischievous; to Mr. Blackman)* (or perhaps even your narrow views of Christ, sir), does that mean I must stay shut up in an insane asylum for the rest of my life?

*(Mr. Blackman and Elizabeth meet eyes. The other trustees exchange looks.)*

MR. BLACKMAN: . . . Mrs. Packard, tell me—in what ways do you differ with the Church, my dear? Do you have visions or hallucinations? Bouts of uncontrollable ravings? Do you speak in tongues?

ELIZABETH *(Laughs)*: No, not in the least. May I describe to you in specific detail my disagreements with my husband's Calvinism—or Puritanism—and my defense of Christianity?

MR. BLACKMAN: Yes, yes, please go ahead.

DR. MCFARLAND: Yes, Mrs. Packard. Please inform the trustees of your . . . very interesting views.

ELIZABETH: Gentlemen, my husband accuses me of teaching my children doctrines . . . ruinous to their spiritual well-being, practices that will endanger their souls for eternity. But, gentlemen, I teach my children Christianity; my husband teaches the children Calvinism. Christianity upholds the authority of salvation and *God*; Calvinism upholds the authority of damnation and the *devil. (Theophilus, outraged: "Where do you—")* Please, hear me out.

MR. BLACKMAN: Mrs. Packard, arc you not bcing nccdlcssly provocative?

DR. MCFARLAND *(Smiling with pleasure)*: Of course she is! She cannot resist.

ELIZABETH: No, no. The intellectual and theological argument will become clear, I promise you, and I think—as men of immense intelligence—you may even find these ideas . . . intriguing, at the very least, sir. *(Mr. Blackman: "I see . . .")* Doctor McFarland did. *(Dr. McFarland sputters: "What? I—I—")*

MR. BLACKMAN *(Flattered by her)*: . . . Well, go on, Mrs. Packard.

ELIZABETH: Calvinism teaches us that our very natures are sinful. Is not this true in your church?

*(The trustees nod and agree.)*

MR. BLACKMAN: Why, yes, of course.

ELIZABETH: From childhood, we are all taught to overcome evil with evil—that is, the very first step towards becom-

ing better is to believe we are *(Mock scolding)* very, very
*bad*! Is this not so?

*(Mr. Blackman smiles, almost laughs, charmed. Theophil-
us is appalled.)*

MR. BLACKMAN: Yes, surely.

ELIZABETH: But Christ taught us to "overcome evil with *good*,"
to *do* good, to take care of our fellow creatures. In fact, he
believed our *true natures* are good. Do you follow me?

MR. BLACKMAN *(Not agreeing, but indulgently allows her to
continue)*: Well . . . yes, continue.

ELIZABETH: Yet my husband preaches that only "the elect" are
good or good enough to be saved! *(Mr. Blackman:
"Surely.")* That election is predestined, and that everyone
who is not "of the elect" will burn in Hell for eternity.
*(Passionately)* Gentlemen, Jesus taught us that we are *all
God's dear children*, and there is no *limit* to God's *mercy*!

MR. BLACKMAN *(Smiling, shaking his head)*: And where does
it tell us this in the Scriptures, Mrs. Packard?

ELIZABETH: I have studied Acts, sir. Chapter 2, Verse 21:
"And it shall come to pass, that whosoever, WHOSO-
EVER, shall call upon the name of the Lord, our God . . .
*shall be saved*." Therefore, repentance always remains a
condition of pardon . . . In other words, we can *all* enter
the Kingdom of Heaven *together*.

MR. BLACKMAN *(Gruff)*: I see . . .

ELIZABETH: Gentlemen, I believe Christ's Word is simple.
Our God is a *nurturing* God—like a mother's love—
rather than a punishing God, and *this* is what I have
taught my children . . . *(Tears streaming)* Simply this . . .
*(Pause)* I am not mad; I merely disagree with my husband,

as many sane wives often do. *(She and Mr. Blackman almost laugh together)* I do not ask my husband to change his beliefs, sir, merely to allow me the right to follow my own . . . *(Quits while she's ahead)* And I—thank you, so very much, for hearing me today.

*(Alarmed, Theopilus and Dr. McFarland exchange glances. Dr. McFarland moves in.)*

DR. MCFARLAND: Is that all you have to say, Mrs. Packard?

ELIZABETH: Yes, that should suffice, Doctor.

DR. MCFARLAND: Mr. Blackman, I—

MR. BLACKMAN *(Gesturing to Dr. McFarland to wait)*: I should likc to thank you, Mrs. Packard. Though I cannot for onc moment sanction your characterization of Calvinism, or Puritanism, you have presented a cogent and *(With irony) mostly* rational treatise on the subject. *(The trustees are amused. Dr. McFarland: "Mr. Blackman, I—")* Gentlemen, I cannot but say Mrs. Packard appears to me far from violent or hopelessly insane. She is certainly emotional— perhaps passionate is more the word—but she is also logical, in her own way, much like my own wife. *(The trustees laugh)* If this is the cause of her confinement here, I, for one, cannot support her staying here . . . *(Elizabeth holds her breath. Dr. McFarland and Theophilus exchange glances)* Don't you concur, gentlemen?

A TRUSTEE: Yes, yes . . . I agree, Mr. Blackman.

DR. MCFARLAND: Mr. Blackman, with all due respect—

MR. BLACKMAN: My own wife, I'm afraid, has been reading far too much for her own good, like Mrs. Packard, and has come up with notions I find to be crack-pot, but I should not like to live without her! *(The trustees laugh)* Doctor

McFarland, I think she should be sent home, though I do not altogether envy the poor reverend's living situation. *(More laughter from the trustees)* He must try to preach one doctrine in his church while his wife preaches another at home and across town! *(More laughter)*

THEOPHILUS: Pardon me, gentlemen. May I say *one word?*

MR. BLACKMAN: Of course, Mr. Packard. First, though, I should like to finish the discussion with your wife, without interruption. Then we can speak together, at length.

THEOPHILUS *(Nods, angry and humiliated)*: I see.

MR. BLACKMAN: Mrs. Packard, is there anything more you should like to add?

ELIZABETH: Only this—I am so very grateful to you, gentlemen, for recognizing my sanity; and thank you, Doctor, for allowing me to present some of my more *(With veiled irony)* . . . "radical" views to the trustees.

DR. MCFARLAND *(Acidly to Elizabeth)*: Indeed. *(To Mr. Blackman and the trustees)* Gentlemen, perhaps we could have a private conference before we speak further with the Packards? Mrs. Packard's illness can be difficult to detect, and she has not accurately described her more—

MR. BLACKMAN *(Piercing; to Dr. McFarland)*: No, I think not, Doctor. Incarceration seems to have been obtained in consequence of Mrs. Packard *using* her reason and, not as reported, by her *losing* her reason. Reverend Packard . . . I should like to hear your thoughts regarding your wife's presentation.

THEOPHILUS: . . . The questioning of doctrine is not worthy of discussion.

MR. BLACKMAN: Well . . . Reverend, as you can see, it does not seem appropriate to me nor to the rest of the trustees here to keep your wife at Jacksonville in either the violent ward

or the 7th Ward any longer. *(Pointedly)* Doctor McFarland
agrees. *Do you not, Doctor?*

DR. MCFARLAND *(Choosing his words extremely carefully)*: . . .
I think the kind of cure Reverend Packard seeks—did
rightly seek—is not possible to attain in this instance.

THEOPHILUS: You concede defeat, Doctor?

DR. MCFARLAND: I am afraid I must, Reverend. I am sorry.
I could not reach her.

MR. BLACKMAN: Could you not, Reverend, find a way to make
peace with your wife—agree to let her think her own
thoughts—these . . . liberal thoughts, as wrong-headed as
you may find them—but confine her speaking about them
to the privacy of your own home? We could make it a condition of her release that she must agree not to speak out
publicly.

THEOPHILUS: I am afraid that is not good enough. She endan-
gers the salvation of the children, gentlemen! May I remind
you that intellectual and moral perversity are forms of
insanity and require confinement?

MR. BLACKMAN: Mr. Packard—

THEOPHILUS: Sir, my wife still holds fast to her heretical ideas.
You have heard, unfortunately, only a very few of her less
radical views. May I describe some of them to you, *please?*

MR. BLACKMAN: That will not be necessary, sir. *(Theophilus:
"Gentlemen, my wife believes—")* Your wife seems to all of
us far from violently insane, and no liberal religious
views—as silly as they are—will change my mind.

THEOPHILUS: Gentlemen, understand—I am a minister of the
old school. My wife did destroy my congregation . . . She
did destroy the very foundation of our marriage and family life. Furthermore, if the kinds of ideas she has adopted
in the past few years—these "liberal ideas" as you call

them—are allowed and encouraged to flourish, they will endanger, I fear, the very foundation of this *country*! May I remind you, gentlemen, that our country was *founded* on exactly those princip—

MR. BLACKMAN: Mr. Packard! *(He puts up his hand to calm him)* —Indeed . . . However, may we return, to the question of your children? For their sakes, Reverend—

THEOPHILUS *(Rising)*: No, no . . . For the sake of my children, sir, I will protect them from their mother's moral degeneracy. As a man of God, I will not, as you seem to want me to do—I will not allow her heretical ideas to infect my home, and I will not *live* a lie. Shame on you, gentlemen. *Shame.*

*(The lights change. Mrs. Blessing testifies.)*

MRS. BLESSING: I lived across the street from the Packards, and it was a madhouse—doors locked, children crying—shameful! One day after Mrs. Packard came back from the asylum, little Isaac came to my house crying, "They are killing my mother." I rushed over there with him and tried to see her, but Mr. Packard refused to let me in. I never thought Mrs. Packard was insane. Mrs. Packard merely claimed the right to live with her family, and considered herself more capable of taking care of her children than any other person. I thought she should divorce, but she knew she would lose her children if she did, and she could not live with that. She said she "wanted protection in her own home, not a complete divorce *from* it."

*(The lights change. The nursery in the Packard home. Theophilus nails the window shut from the inside. It is*

*winter, freezing. Elizabeth is wrapped in a shawl to keep warm.)*

ELIZABETH *(Quiet)*: The irony is not lost on me, Husband, that I have left one prison only to be thrown into solitary confinement in my own home on my release. And in the empty nursery . . .

*(He pounds with the hammer. He does not speak to her. She gets up.)*

Theo, there is no fresh food in the house. Let me go to the market, or send one of the older children. *(He continues hammering)* They are hungry. *(He refuses to answer)* Husband! Please. Let me speak to the children. They know I am here, Theophilus. *(No response)* Why won't you speak to me? They want their mother.

*(The following are the first words he has said to her in days. They tear out of him, the pain is almost unbearable.)*

THEOPHILUS *(Between gritted teeth)*: Stop . . . chattering!

*(Arthur, age five, starts to cry for his mother behind the door.)*

ARTHUR *(From off)*: *Momma, Momma?*
ELIZABETH: Arthur, is that you?

*(Theophilus turns to her in a fury, almost in tears. Then he takes an enormous key chain out of his pocket.)*

THEOPHILUS: There is no money for fresh food.

ELIZABETH: Theophilus, how are we to *live*?

*(He just stares at her. Then he opens the door. Arthur is there. He tries to run to his mother.)*

THEOPHILUS: Come on, Arthur. Come with me. *(Gently)* You cannot see your mother now.

ARTHUR: Are you my momma?

*(As Theophilus takes him off and locks the door:)*

ELIZABETH: Yes! I'm your momma! . . .

*(We hear Arthur, off, calling for his mother. Then silence. A minute later there is a knock on the door. Then a sheet of paper, a letter, is slipped under the door.)*

LIBBY: Read this. You have to read this. Mummy? . . .

ELIZABETH *(Quiet; through the door to Libby)*: Yes, yes. I have it. Thank you, darling.

THEOPHILUS *(From off)*: Libby! Libby! Get away from that door! Now! . . . I am warning you.

*(Elizabeth picks up the letter and reads it. She is shocked by its contents.)*

ELIZABETH *(To herself)*: Oh . . . dear . . . God . . . *(Libby cries)* Don't cry now. Libby, wait here one moment!

*(Elizabeth grabs a pen from the window seat. She scrawls on the envelope.)*

THEOPHILUS: Libby, get away from that door! Do I have to come and get you?

LIBBY: Coming, Pa! Coming!

*(Elizabeth slips the envelope under the door to Libby.)*

ELIZABETH *(Through the door, to Libby)*: Take this message to Mrs. Blessing across the street, all right?

LIBBY: Yes, I will . . .

ELIZABETH: Thank you, Libby dear. You did well. Very well . . . Go on.

*(Elizabeth hears a commotion in the house: doors slamming, drawers slamming. Theophilus screams at the children:)*

THEOPHILUS *(From off)*: Who has been rifling through the mail on my desk?! Isaac?! Libby?!

THE CHILDREN *(From off)*: It wasn't me, it wasn't me . . .

THEOPHILUS *(From off)*: Whoever has stolen a letter from my desk will be severely punished.

*(Theophilus unlocks the door. He enters the nursery and looks around, frantic.)*

ELIZABETH: Looking for this? *(She shows him the letter)*

*(Theophilus stops.)*

THEOPHILUS: Where did you get that? Who—

ELIZABETH: I don't think that is the proper question to ask, Husband. And I would not tell you if I knew. The real question is in regards to the content of this letter. When

did you and your sister plan to have me committed to
*(Reads)* "The Northampton, Massachusetts, Asylum for
the Insane"? *(No answer)* I see. How were you planning
to do it, just out of curiosity? Bind and gag me and carry
me from Illinois to Massachusetts in a private railway car
perhaps? No, too expensive. And you have no money.
Perhaps trick me somehow into thinking all was forgiven,
move to Massachusetts, set up a sweet home near the asylum, and repeat the same kind of kidnapping you did
here? Whatever your scheme, I am sure you and your sister had great fun dreaming it up, and you reveled in the
idea that this time you might be able to get away with it
completely.

THEOPHILUS *(Tears in his eyes, enraged)*: What do you want
from me, Elizabeth? Clearly—God *forgive* me—I've failed
to save you.

ELIZABETH: Oh, is that what you wanted to do?

THEOPHILUS: Yes! That is what I want to do. Do you want to
make me mad? Is that your goal? You have succeeded in
utterly destroying me, the children, and what little professional and family life I managed to maintain in your absence.

ELIZABETH: Self-pity is an ugly emotion, Mr. Packard.
Practice to rid yourself of it. You did make your own
destruction.

THEOPHILUS *(Clear truth)*: Perhaps, but who did make the
children's destruction, Elizabeth? You have hurt the children, I fear, beyond repair.

*(She cannot answer. Long pause.)*

Libby cries and frets all day and cannot sleep at night. The
boys are . . . uncontrollable! You are a selfish and worth-

less mother. Can't you see the children are better off without you?

*(She is wounded to the quick. Theophilus starts for the door.)*

ELIZABETH *(In pain, in rage; hoarsely quiet)*: God sees you,
Theophilus. God hears you, and God will judge you for a
*liar*! What an awful doom awaits you on Judgment Day.

THEOPHILUS: How dare you speak to a man of God in such a
manner?

ELIZABETH: A man of God? Whose God?! There is not an
ounce of compassion in you. You do not believe for one
instant that I am mad. Admit it.

THEOPHILUS: I will not admit to a lie.

ELIZABETH: Nor will I. My mother always thought you cold.
Little did she know how *very* cold.

*(Long pause.)*

THEOPHILUS *(Quiet)*: Your mother . . . was mad. . . . just as you
are.

*(Theophilus exits, slamming the door and locking it.
Elizabeth sits in her rocker and rocks.
    The lights change.)*

JUDGE: Doctor McFarland, you may read your letter into
evidence.

DR. MCFARLAND *(Reads)*: ". . . Your Honor, it is the opinion of
the medical faculty of the Illinois State Hospital for the
Insane at Jacksonville that Mrs. Elizabeth P. W. Packard is
hopelessly insane. Though she can at times appear ratio-

nal, she is in fact delusional and has torn Mr. Packard's life
to pieces. It is my opinion that Mrs. Packard is beyond
hope of being cured, and I will *never*! take her back . . . We
shall not ever . . . readmit her to Jacksonville." My col-
leagues and I have so signed.

*(The lights change. Theophilus enters carrying Elizabeth's
coat.)*

THEOPHILUS: What have you done? What have you done?
Will you ruin everything I touch? Do I count for nothing?
ELIZABETH: What? What's happened?
THEOPHILUS: It seems you somehow, Elizabeth, got a mes-
sage—delivered to Mrs. Blessing across the street?! . . . Is
this true?

*(She smiles.)*

ELIZABETH: Oh. yes . . .
THEOPHILUS: Well, it appears Mrs. Blessing delivered your
message to a *judge*! I have been issued a *writ of habeas cor-
pus*. You and I must appear before a judge in two hours time.

*(He throws her coat at her.)*

Get dressed.

*(He exits. As she puts on her coat:
The lights change. The courtroom.)*

JUDGE: Gentlemen of the jury, let me remind you—though it
is legal for a man to commit his wife to a lunatic asylum

without proof of insanity, it is illegal to imprison a woman in her own home unless she is proven insane in a court of law. Mrs. Packard, I have granted your request to read a short statement to the jury.

ELIZABETH: "Your Honor . . . Gentlemen of the Jury, you have heard all the evidence. I beg you to follow the dictates of your own conscience, God's secretary within you. It is almost by accident that I appear before you. How mysterious are God's ways and plans! . . . God saw that suffering for my opinions was necessary to confirm me in them. And the work is done, and well done, as all God's work always is. I am not now afraid of being called insane if I avow my belief that Christ died for *all* mankind. Can I ever believe God loves his children less than I do mine? Further, because I view Doctor McFarland and my husband differently from how they wish to view themselves, should I therefore be silenced? In America we are a free people, and every citizen living under this government has a right to form his own opinions, and, having formed them, he has a right to express his individual opinions wherever he may think proper. In America, we do not lock up those with whom we disagree. And whosoever seeks to do so is a traitor to our flag and the cause which it represents. Gentlemen of the jury, for those of you who love liberty and for those of you who love women, I entrust my *life* to your good judgment and your manly protection."

JUDGE: Gentlemen, the quality of your service is reflected in your judgment.

*(Gavel.*

*The lights change. Arthur runs to Elizabeth and buries himself in his mother's arms.)*

ELIZABETH: Oh, my darling boy! A last, at last . . .

*(Theophilus comes to take the child. Elizabeth hugs Arthur tight. She meets eyes with Theophilus.)*

*(To Theophilus)* He says you are taking him away. Where are you taking him?

THEOPHILUS: I am taking him *home*, Mrs. Packard. Come along, Arthur.

ELIZABETH *(Into Arthur's eyes)*: Remember: Momma loves you, always. I will be with you . . . as soon as I possibly can . . .

THEOPHILUS: Come away from your mother. You are in my charge.

ELIZABETH: Go with Papa, dear, go on . . . it's all right.

*(Arthur takes Theophilus's hand. Elizabeth tries not to cry.)*

THEOPHILUS: I shall . . . always pray for your soul, Elizabeth . . .

*(Theophilus exits with Arthur.*
*The lights change.)*

JUDGE: Has the jury reached a verdict?

FOREMAN: We have, Your Honor.

JUDGE: The defendant will rise. Mr. Foreman, you may read the verdict.

*(Elizabeth rises, shaky and uneasy.)*

FOREMAN: We, the undersigned jurors in the case of *Packard v. Packard*, having heard the evidence, are satisfied that said Elizabeth P. W. Packard . . . is sane.

*(Elizabeth gasps.)*

JUDGE: It is hereby ordered that Mrs. Elizabeth P. W. Packard be relieved of all restraints incompatible with her condition as a sane woman and is now *at liberty.*

*(Gavel. The court exits. Dr. McFarland approaches Elizabeth.)*

DR. MCFARLAND: My congratulations, Mrs. Packard.
ELIZABETH *(Nods; icy)*: Doctor . . .

*(Long pause. They regard each other. Finally:)*

I was surprised at your veracity on the stand.
DR. MCFARLAND: Pardon me?
ELIZABETH: One of your statements was in fact correct.
DR. MCFARLAND: Oh? And what statement was that, Mrs. Packard?
ELIZABETH: "Mrs. Packard is beyond hope of being cured." That is quite accurate, Doctor. Since I was imprisoned for speaking out, the cure was to silence me, and you failed. I am *in*curable . . . and grateful for it. Now if you will excuse me, I need to see my children— *(Starts to exit)*
DR. MCFARLAND: . . . Mrs. Packard . . . Mr. Packard wanted you to have this. *(He hands her a letter)*
ELIZABETH *(Suddenly alarmed)*: Do you know what's in it?
DR. MCFARLAND *(Sad)*: Oh, yes.
ELIZABETH *(With dread)*: Be merciful. Tell me what it says. *(She steels herself)*
DR. MCFARLAND: . . . Mr. Packard has left for Massachusetts with the children and all your household goods. *(She*

*starts to leave)* No, no. You cannot stop him; he has only taken what is his. The house will be sold. He has left your trunk from the asylum there . . . so you can have some things.

ELIZABETH *(Nodding)*: . . . He has robbed me of everything, except my life. Except my life. *(Struggling)* To have God's approval is now my sole ambition . . . Rest assured, Doctor, I shall put the contents of my trunk to good use.

*(Pause.)*

DR. MCFARLAND: Perhaps we shall make peace in Heaven, Mrs. Packard.

*(She takes his hand. He gently pulls away, then exits.*
*The lights change. A bare stage except for the trunk. Elizabeth moves to the trunk with purpose. She opens it, takes out the mirror and bonnet. Tears streaming, she takes out clothes, rips their seams, pulls out pages of writing from their linings and the lining of the trunk. She continues this as the ensemble enters.)*

MRS. CHAPMAN: It took Elizabeth nine years to gain custody of her children. She and her husband never lived together again.

MRS. STOCKTON: Mrs. Packard died at the age of eighty-one.

MRS. TENNEY: Until the end of her life, she worked for the rights of the mentally ill and partnered with the abolitionists to fight for the emancipation of married women. Her father publicly supported her in her work.

MRS. STOCKTON: Due to her efforts and the influence of her books, thirty-four bills were passed in various legislatures.

"No woman of her day," her obituary read, "except possibly Harriet Beecher Stowe, exercised a wider influence in the interest of humanity."

MR. BLESSING: Mrs. Packard succeeded in having Jacksonville Insane Asylum investigated for negligence and abuse.

MR. BLACKMAN: Though the investigators recommended the firing of Doctor McFarland, the trustees chose not to ask for his resignation.

MRS. STOCKTON: Mrs. Stockton

MRS. CHAPMAN: and Mrs. Chapman

MRS. STOCKTON: died at Jacksonville.

MRS. BONNER: Mrs. Bonner was committed to the poor house for the criminally insane.

THEOPHILUS: Theophilus Packard remained a minister, but never again had his own church. He died at the age of eighty-three. Of all his children, only Samuel lived a long life and was a practicing Calvinist. Arthur and Isaac committed suicide.

LIBBY: Libby lived with her mother until her mother died. Libby died a year later, in an insane asylum.

*(Dr. McFarland enters.)*

DR. MCFARLAND: Doctor McFarland and Mrs. Packard never saw each other again. In 1891, Doctor McFarland . . . hanged himself.

*(We hear the ghostly sound of a prison door slamming shut. Elizabeth looks up.)*

END OF PLAY

EMILY MANN will celebrate her twentieth anniversary as Artistic Director of the McCarter Theatre Center in fall 2009. Ms. Mann wrote and directed *Having Our Say*, adapted from the book by Sarah L. Delany and A. Elizabeth Delany with Amy Hill Hearth, which had its world premiere in 1995 at the McCarter prior to its successful run on Broadway, a national tour and a production at the Market Theatre in Johannesburg, South Africa. In 1995 the Broadway production was nominated for three Tony awards, an Outer Critics Award and a Drama Desk Award. Ms. Mann also wrote the teleplay for *Having Our Say*, which aired on April 18, 1999 as a Kraft Premiere Movie on CBS TV. It received a Peabody Award, a Christopher Award and a nomination for outstanding achievement in television and radio by the Writers Guild of America.

Ms. Mann wrote and directed *Meshugah*, adapted from the story by Isaac Bashevis Singer, which had its world premiere in 1998 at the McCarter and was produced Off-Broadway by Naked Angels. Her play, *Greensboro: A Requiem*, had its world premiere at the McCarter in 1997. Her latest play *Mrs. Packard* premiered at the McCarter in May 2008 and moved to The Kennedy Center in Washington, D.C., under the auspices of The Kennedy Center's Fund for New American Plays.

She received an OBIE Award in 2003 for her direction of the New York run of Edward Albee's *All Over* with Rosemary Harris.

Ms. Mann made her Broadway debut in 1986 as a playwright and director with *Execution of Justice,* for which she received a Bay Area Theatre Critics Award, a Playwriting Award from the Women's Committee of the Dramatists Guild, a Burns Mantle Yearbook Best Play Citation and a Drama Desk nomination. Her play *Still Life* premiered at the Goodman Theatre, and opened Off-Broadway under her direction in 1981, winning six OBIE Awards, including Distinguished Playwriting and Distinguished Directing.

Her first play, *Annulla, An Autobiography,* premiered at The Guthrie Theater in 1977 and was produced at The New Theatre of Brooklyn with Linda Hunt in 1988.

A recipient of the prestigious Hull-Warriner Award and the Edward Albee Last Frontier Directing Award, Ms. Mann is a member of the Dramatists Guild and serves on its Council. She received an Honorary Doctorate of Fine Arts from Princeton University. A collection of her plays, *Testimonies: Four Plays* (including *Annulla, Execution of Justice, Greensboro: A Requiem, Still Life*), has been published by Theatre Communications Group.